Motorbooks International
WARBIRD HISTORY

LOCKHEED
P-38 LIGHTNING

Motorbooks International
WARBIRD HISTORY

LOCKHEED
P-38 LIGHTNING

Steve Pace

DEDICATION

For my dad, James J. "Jim" Gallagher, with all the love and respect any son could generate.

First published in 1996 by Motorbooks International Publishers & Wholesalers, 729 Prospect Avenue, PO Box 1, Osceola, WI 54020-0001 USA

Motorbooks International books are also available at discounts in bulk quantity for industrial or sales-promotional use. For details write to Special Sales Manager at the Publisher's address

Library of Congress Cataloging-in-Publication Data Available

ISBN 0-7603-0151-4

Pace, Steve.
    Lockheed P-38 Lightning / Steve Pace.
       p. cm. -- (Motorbooks International warbird history)
    Includes bibliographical reference and index.
    ISBN 0-7603-0151-4 (alk. paper)
    operations, American. I. Title. II. Series.
    UG1242. F5P317   1996
    358.4'3--dc20   96-9391

On the front cover: *California Cutie*, a beautifully restored P-38, powers into a climbing bank high above the clouds. *John Dibbs*

Back cover, top: Famed Lockheed test pilot Tony LeVier was not afraid to get his hands dirty. Here he his working on the top left-hand engine of a P-38J. *Lockheed Martin*

Back cover, bottom: Pictured here during its first flight with Milo Burcham at the controls, *Yippee* (s/n 44-23296) was a P-39J-20-LO and the 5,000th Lightning built. *Lockheed Martin*

Printed in the United States of America

CONTENTS

ACKNOWLEDGMENTS AND FOREWORD

This book could not have been produced without the help of the individuals as follows: Tony LeVier (retired) and Denny Lombard, Lockheed Martin Skunk Works; Eric Schulzinger and Jim Ragsdale, Lockheed Martin Corporation; Mark Adamic; SMsgt Bob Beggs, HQ 1 FW/HO; Bob Dorr; Jeff Ethell; Eric Falk and Frank Wagner, General Electric Aircraft Engines; Rene Francillon, Air Fan International; Dave Ostrowski; Dr. Ray Puffer,. AFFTC/HO; Ray Wagner, San Diego Aerospace Museum; Dan Whitney; Dennis Wrynn; Mike Haenggi and the rest of the staff at Motorbooks International.

In the early years of World War II, there was one fighter plane that stood out above all others. It was a design so spectacular in appearance, it instantly attracted the attention of everyone that had the pleasure of seeing it flash through the southern California skies.

It had a rare beauty that was unmatched and a sound so smooth and quiet, one might easily miss its approach toward them and it would be long gone. But the after-sound left the viewer quite stunned with a paralyzing astonishment and/or disbelief.

It was so fast you had to see it coming on its approach toward you, or you would miss seeing it zoom upward and out of sight to more than 20,000 feet in a matter of a few minutes. Seeing it was indeed an awesome experience.

I had heard about this fantastic fighter plane long before I joined Lockheed. It had been designed by Clarence L. Johnson, more fondly called "Kelly." His design was the winner of a military requirement for an advanced Interceptor Pursuit.

War clouds had been brewing in Europe for several years, and finally in 1939, all hell broke loose when Hitler and his thugs invaded Poland. America at the time was so unprepared in all areas of military might for a major world confrontation, the P-38 almost overnight became the first most vital fighter plane to the United States and its eventual allies. The U.S. Army Air Corps was so anxious to show off the XP-38's incredible performance, they launched it on a transcontinental speed dash eventhough it had hardly been tested.

Unfortunately, the Allison V-1710 engines faltered during the approach for landing at Mitchel Field, New York, and it crash landed on an adjacent golf course. Though a new speed record had been unofficially recorded, the one-of-a-kind XP-38 was lost. The local military officials could have had the remains of the plane recovered and repaired, but they did not do so.

Lieutenant Benjamin S. Kelsey, the pilot, was so thrilled by the performance and flying qualities of this new bird, he pleaded with the military high command to continue on with the P-38 program with his classic statement: "It flies swell and goes like hell!"

Wisely, the decision of the air corps was to order thirteen service-test YP-38s for further evaluation. As it turned out, that decision was never regretted.

I arrived at Lockheed on 29 April 1941 with great expectation to fly this new Super Fighter. My flying background included aerial racing and aerobatic flying, the perfect credentials for being an experimental airplane test pilot.

Pilots fell in love with it from the very start of its entry into military service. And importantly, its counter-rotating engines and propellers eliminated torque, which was the scourge of piston-powered propeller-driven fighter pilots.

And it was a fighter! Firing its four .50cal machine guns and its single 20mm cannon against a target was literally like shooting fish in a barrel. . . . you couldn't miss!

But with all of its plus factors, there were several alarming deficiencies that were to baffle Lockheed engineers and test pilots for a long time. The first alarm to ring was the P-38's high-speed buffeting at high-altitude, followed by a strong tendency for it to nose-under into an uncontrollable dive.

Kelly Johnson and his top engineers used every resource known to determine the cause of the Lightning's strange misbehavior. The military and other outside experts thought it was the tail surfaces that were at fault and voiced their opinions freely. Then suddenly, disaster struck us a nasty blow which nearly sank the P-38 program. During a dive test with a new "spring tab" on the elevator, the number one YP-38 service test plane dove into the ground in Glendale, California, just a few miles from Lockheed's Burbank factory. Its pilot, Ralph Virden, was killed. Soon after, in another YP-38 dive test, an air corps major named Signa Gilkey was killed.

Events happened so fast after those accidents, it's almost impossible to recount them all in this foreword to Steve Pace's outstanding story of one "Helluva Great Fighter Plane!" So I'm now signing off, but to relieve your curiosity, I did checkout in the P-38 and went on to do most all of the developmental flight-test of the P-38/F-4/F-5 aircraft through the remaining years of the war.

Tony LeVier

Lockheed Aircraft Corporation initially hired Tony LeVier to ferry Hudson bombers to Montreal, Canada, for intended deliveries to the British Royal Air Force. LeVier, who started his long flying career in 1928 at the age of fifteen, soon became an engineering test pilot in 1941 and conducted extensive flight-test evaluations on the P-38 program—specifically, on the Allison engine/General Electric turbosupercharger development, and, dive tests to solve the compressibility problem being faced by these aircraft.

LeVier later made the first flight on the XP-80A, as well as its subsequent Phase I development tests. He was promoted to chief engineering test pilot in 1945. He made the first flight on the Lockheed Saturn in 1946; the first flight as copilot on the Lockheed Constitution in 1946; the first flight on the T-33A (TF-80C earlier) in 1948; and supervised the test pilot programs on all versions of the production Lightnings and Photo Lightnings, F-80 Shooting Stars, Saturns, Constitutions, Constellations, and Neptunes.

LeVier then made the first flight on the XF-90 in 1949; the flights on the F-94A, F-94B, and F-94C Starfire series respectively in 1948, 1949, and 1951; the XF-104 Starfighter in 1954; and the then super-secret U-2 spy plane in 1955.

Shown seated in the cockpit of an F-104 Starfighter is former chief engineering test pilot and director of flying operations Tony LeVier. *Lockheed Martin*

LeVier became director of flying operations at Lockheed in May 1955, and served in that capacity until April 1974, when he retired after 33 years of faithful duty.

Born on 14 February 1913 in Duluth, Minnesota (ironically the very same year Lockheed was founded), Tony LeVier has in excess of 10,000 flying hours and more than 24,000 flights in 260 different types of aircraft. He is a member of the Aviation Hall of Fame, and is the founder and president of Safe Action in Flight Emergency (SAFE). He holds many awards and aviation-related memberships. Finally, LeVier is highly regarded by his peers as a pilot's pilot. He currently resides in La Canada, California.

Steve Pace

INTRODUCTION

Lockheed Aircraft Corporation chief engineer Hall L. Hibbard and his assistant Clarence L. Johnson applied for and received a U.S. patent for their co-inventing effort on the P-38 Lightning. A classic design in the truest sense, the P-38 began life as the most advanced pursuit interceptor aircraft in the world. So advanced in fact that when the U.S. Army Air Corps started receiving its thirteen service test YP-38s for evaluations in late 1940, it immediately realized that the airplane was extremely dangerous to those individuals who ignored the pilot's manual. Simply stated: if you didn't know how to fly it, before you flew it, you blew it!

The Army Air Corps found the YP-38s to be very fast with their 400 mph speed at 20,000 feet and were amazed at their ability to climb 3,330 feet in a single minute: that is, they could reach 20,000 feet in a mere six minutes. And with its maximum range of 1,150 miles on 410 gallons of fuel, it proved to be a long-range asset as well. It was an airplane with no equal.

Powered by two V-12 piston engines spinning three-bladed propellers in opposing directions to eliminate the effects of torque on its airframe, production P-38s proved to be highly agile and maneuverable.

Having produced forty-one aces with at least five kills each—including America's two top scoring aces—the P-38 was respected by those who flew it and by those who fought it.

Called the "fork-tailed devil" by the Germans and the "plane with two tails" by the Japanese, the Lightning was a true dogfighter.

Following an Army Air Corps contract award in 1937 to produce a new pursuit airplane—the XP-38—Lockheed completed its work, and on 27 January 1939, the first P-38 took to the air. With its 400 mph speed, the XP-38 proved to be 100 mph faster than any other fighter in the world.

Lightning production began in earnest in September 1939, the very same time that war broke out in Europe. By the time fighting was over, Lockheed and Consolidated Vultee had produced 10,038 P-38s in eighteen versions. They served as fighters, fighter-interceptors, fighter-bombers, photographic reconnaissance planes, and in many other categories. Such service earned the airplane a reputation as the most versatile combat aircraft of its day.

Two turbo-supercharged Allison engines and its unique twin-boom design gave the Lightning an inherent ruggedness and the ability to lift heavy loads, including a heavier bomb load than that carried by the early Boeing B-17. When armed with 2,000 rounds of .50 calibre ammunition for its four machine guns and sixty rounds for its 20mm cannon, its concentrated firepower was devastating.

The triple-bodied and double-tailed P-38s are remembered by many as the most successful twin-engined fighters to do battle in World War II. Pilots flying them sank destroyers and submarines. They crippled tanks and locomotives with strafing fire, blew up pillboxes with rockets and bombs, and eliminated hundreds of enemy aircraft. A P-38 was the first American aircraft to shoot down a German plane after the United States entered World War II. In the Pacific, P-38s destroyed the airplane carrying Admiral Isoroku Yamamoto, the architect of the Japanese bombing of Pearl Harbor. U.S. Army Air Force Majors Dick Bong and Tom McGuire, the two top scoring American aces of the war, flew P-38s exclusively. P-38s are credited with more kills of Japanese aircraft than any other U.S. fighter.

A small number of Lightnings flew for China, the Free French, Great Britain, and Portugal. After the war a few P-38s were procured by the air forces of Italy and Honduras. in favor of turbojet-powered fighters, however, including the Lockheed F-80 Shooting Star, the U.S. Air Force quickly scrapped or surplused its fleet of P-38s. In production from 1940 to 1945, with more than 10,000 being produced, the P-38 fought in every theater of operation during the war.

Appropriately named Lightning (lightning does come from the ground) by the British Royal Air Force, the P-38 was a remarkable fighter plane. Working in concert with other great U.S. fighter aircraft the P-38 Lightning played a major role in the allied effort to win World War II. It most certainly is a plane to be remembered.

As USAAF Maj. Dick Long looks on, Milo Burcham points out the new dive-recovery flaps that allowed later P- 38Js and P-38Ls to more safely dive at higher speeds and steeper angles. *Lockheed Martin*

CHAPTER ONE

PROTOTYPES: THE XP- AND YP- 38s

On 17 December 1944—on the forty-first anniversary of the Wright Brother's first powered and controlled flight of an airplane—U.S. Army Air Forces (USAAF) Maj. Richard I. "Dick" Bong acquired his fortieth kill to not only become an ace eight-times over but the Air Force's all-time highest scoring ace. Nine days later, USAAF Maj. Thomas B. "Tom" McGuire Jr. obtained his thirty-eighth kill to emerge as the Air Force's second highest scoring ace. No other Air Force aces, flying any other type of fighter plane, have ever surpassed their marks. These two, and thirty-nine others, all got their aerial victories while flying and fighting in the Lockheed P-38 Lightning during World War II. Yet, as good as all this sounds, this great fighter had an awkward genesis.

It all began on 14 February 1937, when Lockheed and five other airframe contractors (Boeing, Consolidated, Curtiss, Douglas, and Vultee) were invited to join in on a new U.S. Army Air Corps (USOAC) design competition under Circular Proposal Number 37-X608 to find an advanced pursuit-interceptor airplane. Using an improved B-series General Electric supercharger, the advanced fighter was to be a single-seat type with a minimum level-flight speed of 360 mph and a "wished for" level-flight speed of

Powered by two 1,150 horsepower Allison V-1710-11/-15 C-series engines with exhaust-driven General Electric B-2 turbosuperchargers, the XP-38 poses on a ramp at what is now March AFB some nine miles southeast of Riverside, California. Without any telltale sign of engine exhaust on the engine nacelle's cowling, it appears this photo was taken prior to its first flight. Note the extremely pointed propeller hub spinner tried early on to help eliminate unwanted parasite drag; found unnecessary, less pointed and more rounded spinners were later used. *Dave Ostrowski Collection*

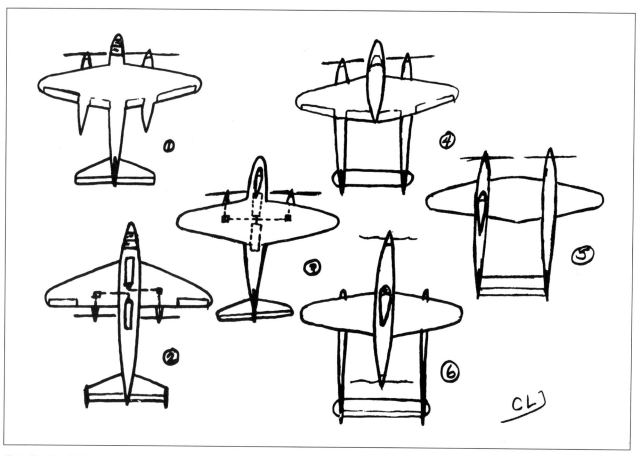

The Lockheed Model 2264-01 or XP-38 airplane was not designed "on the back of a business envelope" as has been rumored in the past, but these early sketches drawn by Kelly Johnson show an interesting evolution of the varied configurations he and Hall Hibbard considered. It was the number four sketch that resembled most what finally became the XP-38. These sketches were drawn in February 1937, twenty-three months before the XP-38's first flight. *Lockheed Martin*

400 mph or more. As a pursuit-interceptor type of airplane, it was to have a quick time-to-climb capability, going from take-off to 20,000 feet within six minutes, and operate efficiently at or above that altitude. As primarily a bomber-destroyer, it was to be armed with a single rapid-firing cannon.

On 23 June 1937, following the CP No. 37-X608 competition, the USAAC announced that the Lockheed Aircraft Corporation of Burbank, California, had won and a contract would be drawn and approved the same day. The contract (AC-9974) called for the construction and flight-test of one experimental prototype designated XP-38(S/N 37-457), one full-scale engineering mockup, one static structural load-test article, and wind-tunnel models and data.

Production supercharged engines were a scarce commodity in mid-1937. Using a General Electric exhaust-driven Model B-2 unit, the liquid-cooled Allison V-1710 twelve-cylinder engine had a take-off horsepower rating of 1,150. Turbosupercharged then, the Allison V-1710 was the most powerful engine available at the time. Knowing this, Lockheed propulsion engineers recommended the V-1710/B-2 combination to propel the XP-38.

Lockheed had learned earlier about high-altitude flight with its XC-35, a modified Lockheed C-35 Electra. Nicknamed "The Boiler," due to its circular cross-section fuselage, this twin 550 horsepower Pratt & Whitney Wasp–powered airplane likewise used the General Electric B-2 turbosuper-

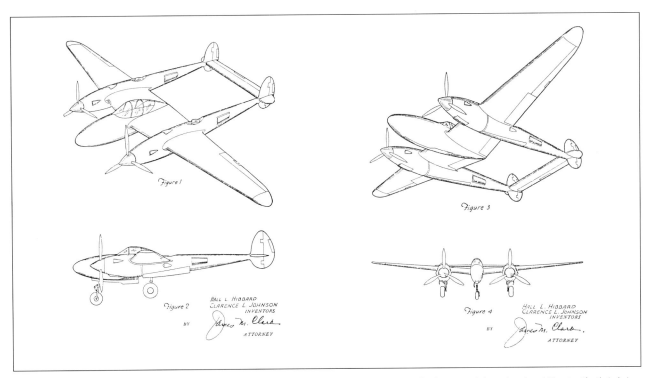

Hall Hibbard, Lockheed chief engineer, and Kelly Johnson, his assistant, co-invented the XP-38. Thus it was necessary for them to apply for and receive a U.S. patent for their design. Here, figure one (upper left) through figure four (lower right), as prepared by their patent attorney James M. Clark, is the actual XP-38 design they patented. *Lockheed Martin*

chargers for its high-altitude engine efficiency. The XC-35 tests were so successful the USAAC was presented the prestigious Robert J. Collier Trophy for its participation in the design and use of equipment critical for a substratosphere airplane. During XC-35 flight-test activities, Lockheed among other things learned about the performance of hydraulic fluid at low temperature, design and operation of automated cabin pressurization controls, and significantly to the future of the P-38, the operating characteristics of turbosupercharged engines.

Developing and Building the XP-38

To develop and build the XP-38, designated in-house as the Model 22, Lockheed set up a small workshop behind locked doors in Burbank. By order of the USAAC, the XP-38 program was to be maintained as a top secret venture due to the aeronautical breakthroughs it might generate.

The information Lockheed engineers had acquired on the high-flying XC-35 and on the supercharged V-1710 provided the knowledge they needed to meet the requirements of the classified X608 project. Their earlier experience gained on the proposed Lockheed XFM-2 likewise prompted Lockheed engineers to come up with a suitable fighter design.

Led by Lockheed chief engineer Hall L. Hibbard and his assistant Clarence L. "Kelly" Johnson, a variety of design concepts were put forth by Lockheed's preliminary design team to match the requirements for the proposed fighter—mainly by Kelly Johnson himself.

In concept one, a very conventional layout, the engines would have been mounted to wing nacelles; in concept two, as a pusher-type, the engines would have been installed in tandem within the fuselage; in concept three, engines installed in tandem within the fuselage, it would have been a tractor-type; in concept four, using a twin-boom arrangement with a central pod housing the cockpit, the engines would be mounted to the front of the booms; in concept five, again using twin-booms, with the cockpit in the left-hand boom, the engines were also mounted to the front of the booms; and in concept six, in a wing-boom to tail-boom arrangement, both engines would have been mounted within the fuselage driving pusher- and tractor-type propellers. Concept four, most logically, was the final choice due to the boom configuration which accommodated all the needs of the pilot, engines, landing gear, armament and its electrical, hydraulic, and fuel systems. Moreover, this arrangement allowed for correct aircraft balance.

As the result of Lockheed's X608 design arrangement, the nose landing gear, armament, and pilot were accommodated in a miniature fuselage mounted on wing centerline. The armament was to be made up of a cannon (20mm or 37mm) and four 0.50 calibre machine guns. Since the fuse-

Successfully flown by Lockheed test pilot Marshall Headle on 17 September 1940 from the Lockheed Air Terminal, Burbank, California, the first of 13 Model 122-62-02 YP-38 service test airplanes is shown during its first take off. The YPs were powered by two F-series 1,150 horsepower V-1710-27/-29 Allison V-12 engines and had a top speed of 413 mph at 20,000 feet—in level flight, 53 mph more than stipulated by the USAAC. Due to its early demise the XP-38 was never armed (it was to carry one 20mm cannon and four .50 calibre machine guns); but the YPs carried a revised armament of one 37mm cannon (fifteen rounds), two .30 calibre machine guns (500 rounds per gun), and two .50 calibre machine guns with 210 rounds per gun. *Dave Ostrowski Collection*

ABOVE AND OPPOSITE
One cannot over emphasize the importance of wind-tunnel evaluations on aircraft—especially when this can be done with a full-size specimen. Here, perched atop pylons in the NACA Langley (now NASA Langley Research Center) Full-Scale Wind-Tunnel is the number two YP-38. In operation since 1931, this all-important wind-tunnel is still being used and, since its inception, has evaluated many notable aircraft. But in this case, it mostly helped evaluate the Lockheed P-38—the world's fastest twin-engine, piston-powered and propeller-driven fighter plane. *NASA Langley Research Center via Keith Henry*

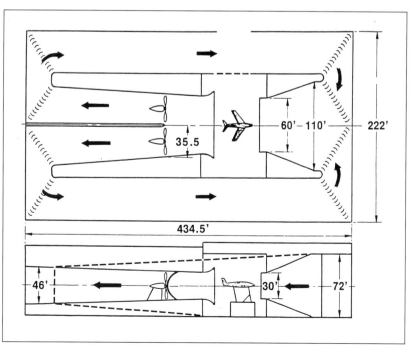

60' - 110'

35.5

222'

434.5'

46'   30'   72'

Neither the XP-38 nor the YP-38s were built at Lockheed's main Burbank factory complex as shown here circa 1940. However by mid-1945, in addition to many other Lockheed types, this complex had produced 9,910 of the 10,038 Lightnings built. *Lockheed Martin via Dennis Wrynn*

lage was not mounted within the arcs of the three-bladed propellers, and the cannon/guns were on aircraft centerline, the fighter would have a concentrated volume of firepower. And since the mini-fuselage held the nose gear, and the main landing gears were attached to either boom, the X608 would become the first fighter with a tricycle landing gear arrangement.

Lieutenant Benjamin S. "Ben" Kelsey, later X608 project test pilot for the USAAC, was convinced of the merits of a tricycle landing gear arrangement. And with the backing of his commander, Gen. Oliver P. Echols, "tricyclegears" were incorporated on the XP-38. As it would turn out, this then new type of landing gear proved to be more than adequate.

The XP-38s other design features were not only necessary but important. Aft of the tri-bladed, constant-speed, full-feathering Curtiss electric propellers, there was enough room for the air-inlet scoops, turbosuperchargers, and the radiator-cooling scoops. The main landing gear wheels would retract into bays aft of the turbosuperchargers and ahead of the radiators. Additionally, there was adequate area for the air-induction and cooling ducts, and for other aircraft components.

As it was configured, the XP-38s propeller slipstreams would generate ram air for cooling, and improved air flow around its two rudders to boost directional control. In this way, the hot coolant was removed from the cockpit area and the fuel would be entirely housed within the wing. Pilot visibility was amplified with the use of a glass windshield with a hatch-type cockpit entry. The cockpit layout itself was spacious, with a control wheel to control pitch and roll.

Importantly, total capability in the use of the plane's internal volume was realized, and its over-all fineness ratio and low frontal area would produce minimal parasite drag.

In April 1937, just three months after it had been made aware of program X608, Lockheed's proposed twin-boomed, twin-tailed Model 22 fighter design was submitted to the USAAC. In part, as proposed by Lockheed: "It was designed to operate at a critical altitude of 20,000 feet and at speeds up to 400 mph." The proposal also notes that the ". . . airplane is to not only be flush riveted [then new], but painted and polished as well." Included within the proposal was a very lengthy discussion of the relationship between skin friction drag and aircraft surface condition. Reference was made and information was used from an article in the April 1936 issue of *Aircraft Engineering* titled "Skin Drag of High Speed Aircraft," by S. Hoerner. Flight experience with drag measurements made on the Lockheed Model 12 Electra was also mentioned. The author of this proposal was none other than the XP-38s designer, Kelly Johnson.

In June 1937, the USAAC announced the two winners of the dual pursuit-interceptor competition—Bell and Lockheed. Bell would build and test a single-engine, single-seat prototype under CP 37-X609, to be designated XP-39 and named Airacobra. Lockheed was to manufacture and test the twin-engined, single-seat prototype under CP 37-X608, now designated XP-38 and, at this time, named Atlanta.

As shown in Table 1-1, the XP-38 was to have the following minimal specifications:

XP-38 Specifications (minimal)

Gross takeoff weight	10,500 pounds
Wing area	327.5 square feet
Wing aspect ratio	8.25:1
Wing loading	32 pounds per square foot
Maximum speed	417 mph @ 20,000 feet
Service ceiling	39,100 feet
Range	1,386 miles / 400 gallons fuel
Landing speed	72.2 mph

Flight-test Activities

According to Dick Foss and Roy Blay in an April 1987 article in *Lockheed Horizons* titled "From Propellers To Jets In Fighter Aircraft Design," many design questions needed resolution before the first flight test in July 1937. This required a very strenuous design and fabrication process, with engineers, technicians, and mechanics all working side-by-

side, inventing, changing, and assembling the design. Wind-tunnel tests had to confirm the wing design and develop the required high-lift system. Slotted Fowler-type flaps were perfected so that the basic high-wing-loading concept desired for mission performance could be kept and still permit low landing speeds. Production techniques had to be revised and improved to achieve the flush butt joints and flush rivet construction that was to be used for the exterior surfaces of the airplane. New materials had to be found to cope with the high exhaust temperature environment encountered by the ducting to the turbosuperchargers.

The XP-38 was completed in eighteen months. After midnight on New Years Eve, 1 January 1939, after most of the parties were over, the disassembled airplane was secretly hauled by truck from Lockheed's experimental shop in Burbank, California, to March Army Air Field (AAF)—now March Air Force Base (AFB)—at Riverside, California. Escorted by Army soldiers and a number of Lockheed plant security guards, the one-of-a-kind airplane arrived safely in early morning. Since Lockheed had no experienced fighter-type test pilots at the time, USAAC Lt. Ben Kelsey, already X608 project test pilot, doubled as Lockheed's XP-38 test pilot. The airplane was assembled and prepared for flight-test.

During taxi tests, Lieutenant Kelsey found braking problems; he actually bent a brake pedal trying to stop the XP-38. After two weeks of interim fixes, the plane's braking system was declared acceptable and it was cleared for its initial flight-test activities at March AAF.

It was now 27 January 1939, and after the highly-polished aluminum-clad XP-38 lifted off, Lieutenant Kelsey flew it for a troubled thirty-four minutes. Just after lift-off, three of the four Fowler flap actuation cylinders broke, which in turn left the flaps fully extended, resulting in a floating condition. Flying in an unfamiliar airplane that was experiencing a heavy buffeting activity, Kelsey thought about bailing out. Instead he convinced himself that sufficient control could be kept for a landing. The chase plane—a Ford Trimotor manned by Lockheed and USAAC personnel—visually verified his plight. Safely on the ground, Kelsey noted that the airplane was for the most part "more than interesting" but "less than adequate."

Following additional fixes with improved brake and Fowler flap parts, subsequent flights were nearly trouble-free. More importantly, the XP-38's high-performance attributes were being quickly realized. So the USAAC opted to ferry the plane to Wright AAF, Dayton, Ohio, for further flight-test evaluations. Due to its then fantastic speed potential, Kelsey was given the green light to make the trip "as fast as he could."

With only about five hours of flight time logged on the airplane, Kelsey departed March AAF on 11 February 1939. The XP-38 landed at Amarillo, Texas, three hours and ten minutes later. After refueling and another two-hour and forty-five minute flight, he landed at Wright AAF.

In attendance was Chief of the USAAC Maj. Gen. Henry H. "Hap" Arnold, who had earlier stipulated that if all went well, Kelsey would continue on to Mitchel AAF, Long Island, New York, to simultaneously set a new transcontinental speed record. Kelsey would later say:

> *General Arnold concurred in the estimate that the delivery flight to Wright Field operated at cruise power would approximate the flight speed of the then existing coast-to-coast record of Howard H. Hughes. Being interested in having a demonstration that American planes were not behind European ones and in using this to take off some of the political heat in Washington, he approved a continuation beyond Dayton to Mitchel Field in New York if the flight to Dayton indicated the possibility of approaching the Hughe's record. Arnold gave the final approval.*

Howard Hughe's record was set on 19 January 1937 when he grabbed the world landplane speed record of 327.1 mph flying his model H-1 single-engine race plane between Burbank, California, and Newark, New Jersey, in seven hours and twenty-five minutes. And of course, with that accomplishment, he tried to sell a fighter version of his H-1 to the USAAC. Not really interested in the Hughes's design, the USAAC wanted to use this opportunity to eliminate the H-1's speed record and viability.

With Arnold's blessing, Kelsey and the XP-38 left Dayton and headed for Mitchel Field. Arriving ahead of time with a total flying time of seven hours and two minutes, and a total elapsed time of seven hours and forty-three minutes, Kelsey entered into the traffic pattern at Mitchel. Not knowing that an attempted speed record was being made (not even an unofficial one), the Mitchel tower radioed the XP-38 to "land number four" behind a trio of Consolidated PB-2As.

Kelsey elected to take a long base-leg run and come in low and slow behind the PB-2As without any landing protest or priority. Suddenly, his engines lost power. Not responding to any of Kelsey's commands, the engines went limp and the XP-38, with a mere flying time of a little more than twelve hours, crashed 2,000 feet short of its destination. Clipping tree tops and coming to rest on a golf course, the airplane was destroyed. Fortunately, Kelsey survived without any injuries.

An intense USAAC crash investigation followed and found that in all probability, due to existing weather conditions in the area, the V-1710's carburetors and/or fuel lines had iced up. This was a cold, hard fact of life that had eliminated a valiant effort to bring into being a new breed of fighter plane that would ultimately go on to become one of the deadliest fighters in World War II.

In spite of its early demise, the XP-38 had proved its worth, convincing the USAAC that Lockheed had more than met their contract performance requirements. It was time to sell the plane to the War Department. With the prompting of General Arnold, Lieutenant Kelsey and others, then Secretary of War Harry H. Woodring agreed, and on 27 April 1939, a contract was issued to Lockheed for thirteen YP-38 service test aircraft.

The YP-38s, powered by updated 1,150hp V-1710-27/-29 engines, featured improved brakes and structural redesign targeted for full-scale production. And unlike the XP-38, which had inward-rotating propellers, the YP-38s came with outward-turning props to reduce torque. This modification alone would make the aircraft much more stable during all phases of flight. Moreover, with the improved F series Allison engine, the aftward-flowing prop wash across the YP-38s' flying surfaces would improve for even better in-flight handling.

Lockheed test pilot Marshall Headle made the first flight of a YP-38 at Burbank on 17 September 1940. Joined by twelve other YP-38s, accelerated and extensive manufacturer and service tests followed. The USAAC took possession of its first ever 400 mph–fighter plane on 11 March 1941, just nine months before the attack on Pearl Harbor.

XP-38 Specifications (actual)

Length	37 feet, 10 inches
Wing span	52 feet
Height	12 feet, 10 inches
Empty weight	11,507 pounds
Gross weight	14,200 pounds
Cruising speed	Unknown
Maximum speed	413 mph @ 20,000 feet
Rate of climb	3,076 feet per minute
Service ceiling*	38,000 feet
Maximum range	1,390 miles
Powerplant	Two 1,150 hp Allison V-1710-11/-15 engines
Armament	None

YP-38 Specifications

Length	37 feet, 10 inches
Wing span	52 feet
Height	9 feet, 10 inches
Empty weight	11,171 pounds
Gross weight	14,500 pounds
Cruising speed	330 mph
Maximum speed	405 mph @ 20,000 feet
Rate of climb	3,333 feet per minute
Service ceiling	38,000 feet
Maximum range	1,150 miles
Powerplant	Two 1150 hp Allison V-1710-27/-29 engines
Armament	Two .30cal machine guns, two .50cal machine guns and one 37 mm cannon

* Service ceiling is the maximum altitude reached where an airplane can no longer climb at least 500 feet per minute.

CHAPTER TWO

POWER UP: THE TWIN V-12S

P-38s were powered by a pair of liquid-cooled, twelve-cylinder Allison V-1710 engines spinning outward-turning (toward either wing tip) three-bladed propellers. Counter-rotating propellers can-celled the torque produced by the spinning engine components, which in turn provided increased sta-bility for machine gun and cannon firings, photo-graphic activities, and bombardment operations. These engines, optimized for high-altitude operation with the General Electric B-series of turbosuper-charger units, allowed the P-38 series of aircraft to exceed 400 mph and 40,000 feet. They made the Lightning one of the most maneuverable and agile fighters of World War II. The following pas-sages by Dan Whitney are excerpts from his book *Vees For Victory*:

These are P-322s being manufactured for the Royal Air Force of Great Britain. Though it wanted them, the RAF was forced to refuse them due to their lack of turbosuperchargers. Without this vital component, the P-322s were inferior to German fighters. *Lockheed Martin via Dennis Wrynn*

By the late 1920s the liquid-cooled engine had reached the point of dominance in the field of high-powered, high-speed aircraft. Setting the stan-dard was the liquid-cooled and supercharged Rolls-Royce R engine, a V-12 belting out 1,900 bhp. Other engine manufacturers were likewise com-mitted to capitalizing on the advantages of these inline smooth-running V-type engines as they were easily adapted to streamlined airframes and offered minimal frontal area for increased speed and opti-mum over-the-nose pilot visibility.

Separately, the U.S. Army Air Corps had been developing a new chemical coolant for its water-cooled inline engines. This was intended to allow higher coolant temperatures, and thereby promised a significant reduction in the frontal

area of the radiators necessary for engine cooling. Such developments were deemed essential if the speeds of current aircraft were ever to be significantly increased. They subsequently converted a number of Curtiss-Wright V-1570 Conqueror liquid-cooled engines to operate on Prestone, the commercial name for ethylene glycol used as the chemical coolant. While the system worked quite well, many problems were experienced due to the inprecise way the Conqueror piston cylinders were constructed and the tendency of Prestone to leak through the smallest passage. What was needed was an engine specifically designed for high-temperature liquid cooling.

The Allison Engineering Company

The Allison Engineering Company of Indianapolis, Indiana, had gotten its start in 1915 doing specialized engineering and manufacturing, primarily for the teams fielding race cars in the Indianapolis 500. During World War I and subsequent they turned their expertise to special projects for the military, and, importantly, built the "pattern" Liberty-12 V-1410 engine used to standardize the engines coming from the various Liberty engine manufacturers. Following the war they developed a respectable business in overhauling and modernizing the Liberty engines. In the process they became intimately familiar with the engine and its poor reliability due to frequent failure of the standard babbitted lead and bronze bearings of the era. In response, Allison chief engineer Norman H. "Norm" Gilman invented and developed a much improved bearing consisting of a steel shell with fine-grained bronze bonded to it. With his bearing the Liberty-12 was able to run five- to ten-times longer, while the safety and reliability of the engine was greatly improved. Thus Allison was soon mass-producing these bearings for most of the U.S. aircraft engine manufacturers, and it was sales of these bearings that made the company profitable.

As a specialty engineering firm with expertise in engines, Allison became involved in other closely related projects. Beginning in the early 1920s they built twelve marine yacht engines of their own design that demonstrated a number of design features and refinements which were to be

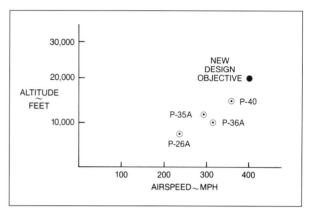

This graph shows the performance of USAAC fighters in the year 1937; new design objective—the black dot above P-40, shows where the Air Corps wanted and needed the P-38 to be. *Lockheed Martin*

carried on to the later V-1710 engine for the P-38 and other aircraft. Also for the USAAC they built the experimental X-4520, a monstrous 24-cylinder air-cooled engine rated at 1,200 bhp. They also built a large number of inverted Liberty engines, mainly to improve saftey and the pilot's forward field of view. These engines were built in both liquid- and air-cooled versions, all normally rated at about 425 bhp.

In August 1918 James J. "Jim" Allison, founder and president of the company, died following a short bout with pneumonia. Due to its innovations and profits, the Allison Engineering Company was eagerly sought by a number of suitors who saw it as an easy ticket into the then rapidly growing aviation field. The successful bidder was none other than Edward "Eddie" Rickenbacker, the leading U.S. ace of World War I with 24.33 kills. (He would later extol the virtues of the P-38 and played a significant role in selling it to the USAAC.)

It was during this period that Norm Gilman was looking for a new product for the company, for the venerable Liberty-12 work was beginning to fade away as it had become ever-more dated. To this end, in late 1928, he designed a new high-temperature liquid-cooled piston cylinder sleeve.

Eddie Rickenbacker ended up selling the company after only a few months to the Fisher Brothers of automotive fame. They encouraged Gilman to proceed with a design for a six-cylinder inline engine

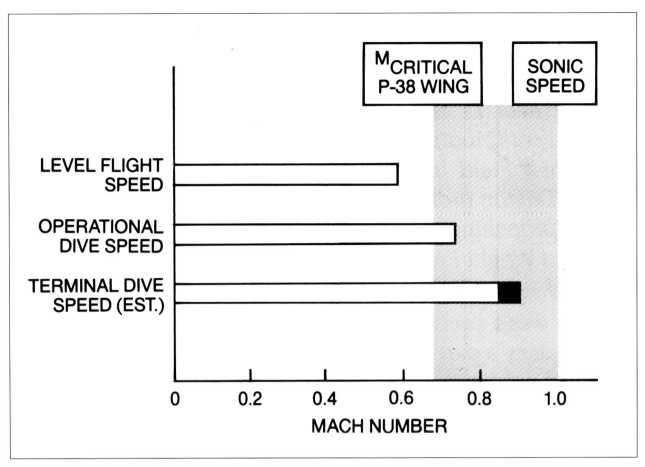

This graph shows the range of P-38 compressibility. That is, its level flight was near Mach number 0.60; its operational dive speed was near Mn 0.70; and its estimated maximum dive speed was near Mn 0.85. According to the USAAF pilot's manual, with dive recovery flaps extended, true indicated air speed was not to exceed 460 mph in a dive from 30,000 feet. *Lockheed Martin*

using his newly designed cylinder intended for use in the burgeoning light airplane market. They in turn sold the company after only three months to the General Motors Corporation. With the encouragement of General Motors, Gilman then ended the six-cylinder project and began the design of a large cubic-inch displacement V-12 engine. This was a prudent move by General Motors, who recognized Allison's experience with liquid-cooled V-12 engines. With the successes being enjoyed by V-12s in automobile racing, and their correct anticipation of the need by the military for a more advanced and higher powered aircraft engine, General Motors had their sights set on producing a V-12 with no equal.

The Early V-1710

Gilman then sketched an engine that he intended to produce 1,000 bhp but to be rated at only 750 bhp as it was then believed that the military would not want or use anything more powerful. The resulting V-12 had 5.5 inch diameter cylinders, each having a stroke of 6 inches. Thus the Gilman-designed V-12 was an engine of 1,710 cubic inches.

All of this was fortunate for the Allison Engineering Company, for with the stock-market crash in October 1929, the strength and support of General Motors was important in keeping the company in business. Furthermore, at an early juncture General Motors agreed to use their own funds to support the development of the V-1710 engine to the point where it could obtain military contracts.

Even though a likely user of the V-1710, the USAAC was not supportive of the project. They were skeptical of Allison's ability and credentials to actually produce a successful home-grown engine. Moreover, with the minimal budgets of the day, they had no funds with which to support the engine. Their one encouragement came in recommending that Allison seek U.S. Navy support for the project, as they believed the U.S. Navy was looking for an engine suitable for a proposed long-range patrol aircraft.

As it developed, Navy interest was actually for an engine to replace the German Maybach engines then powering the large naval airships—the USS *Akron* and USS *Macon*. With this goal, the Navy

On the line at right, P-38s moved aft until they were ready to move forward on the line at left, then out the door you cannot see to your rear. *Lockheed Martin via Dennis Wrynn*

Nearly complete, these P-38s are on their way out of the factory. *Lockheed Martin via Dennis Wrynn*

agreed to procure a single 650 bhp GV-1710A, as it had already been designed by Allison. This was done to expedite development of the engine it really wanted, a 650 bhp reversible engine weighing less than 1,000 pounds.

The Gilman-designed GV-1710A went through two major builds before successfully completing the specified tests in 1932—the engine exceeded the Navy's requirements at 750 bhp. The USAAC witnessed all of the tests and attended most contractor meetings during this period. This led them to begin negotiations with Allison earlier in January 1931 for an engine similar to the GV-1710A, but with the nose case extended 12 inches and equipped with a 2:1 reduction gear suitable for fitting in a streamlined nacelle. (Note: Many references have incorrectly identified this reduction gear as an "epi-cylic" design, which usually has the input and output shafts on the same centerlines. In fact it was an "internally driven spur gear" which has the propeller centerline only slightly above the crankshaft centerline. The USAAC never liked this design as they felt it overloaded the front cheek of the crank-

shaft and caused undue loading on the crankshaft pinion gear as well.)

To this end Allison guaranteed the engine to deliver 750 bhp, but it was detail designed to be capable of 1,000 bhp, and to be suitable for operation with a turbosupercharger. In the meantime, Allison was hard at work building the reversible and normally aspirated (carbureted) engine specifically for use on naval airships. The significant design challenge was to provide the various components necessary to allow the engine to run in either direction, a feature necessary for maneuvering an airship. Allison successfully accomplished the feat and demonstrated these features in the test engine. Two pre-production V-1710Bs (the B suffix meaning reversible) were on the shipping dock, ready to go to the U.S. Navy, on the very same day the USS *Macon* was lost in the Pacific Ocean, just off Monterey, California, on 12 February 1935. Coupled with the previous loss of the USS *Akron*, the U.S. Navy was suddenly out of the large airship business; and so ended their V-1710 engine programs.

Luckily for Allison however, since the USAAC was witness to the V-1710's potential, its future was still bright.

The C Series

Earlier, on 15 June 1933, Allison delivered the first V-1710C engine, USAAC designation XV-1710-1. Allison then initiated the arduous task of supporting the completion of the U.S. Army Air Corps specified 150 hour Military Type Test program. Actual testing was accomplished by the Air Corps Material Division at Wright Army Air Field, Dayton, Ohio. This first engine was able to complete its initial 50 hour qualification test without too much trouble at 800 bhp, so the USAAC elected to procure a second engine—designated XV-1710-3—to be tested at the desired 1,000 bhp rating. This then became the Type Test engine.

Ordered in March 1934, and delivered on 24 June 1934, this engine was to go through many trials and tribulations, running hundreds of hours, but was never able to successfully complete the Type Test without a failure of some sort. Testing continued for almost two years, to April 1936. In anticipation of early qualification of the new engine, the USAAC ordered ten YV-1710-3s for service testing on 18 June 1934. Release for manufacture was to await completion of the 150 hour Military Type Test program with the prototype XV-1710-3 engine.

In an effort to complete the Type Test, one of the ten YV-1710-3s was built to incorporate a number of improvements intended to give the engine the capability to complete the program. This engine was delivered in June 1936 as the YV-1710-7 (also known as the "dash seven"). Amazingly it had been

In another production building, these P-38Js are in final assembly. Note the number one Constellation in the background. It would make its first flight on 9 January 1943. *Lockheed Martin via Dennis Wrynn*

designed and constructed during a frantic thirteen-week effort by a small Allison crew in the spring of 1936. One significant change incorporated into this engine was a newly designed air intake manifold contributed by Allison's new chief engineer, Ronald M. "Ron" Hazen. It greatly improved operation by delivering a uniform amount of air/fuel mixture to the twelve widely separated cylinders. This new manifold resolved many of the previous problems, which had been caused by mixture unevenness resulting in hot cylinders and pistons, warped valves, and some tendency toward untimely detonations. Though improved and enlarged on future

models, the ram-type intake manifold was at the heart of what became the smooth-running series of Allison V-1710 engines.

The dash seven had successfully completed 141 hours of the 150 hour Type Test evaluation when the right cylinder head cracked in the middle, followed by a similar failure of the left head. Allison engineers quickly redesigned the cylinder head to "bullet-proof" the affected area of the head and, with a few other improvements from lessons learned during these tests, reconfigured the dash seven engine to continue the Type Test program.

A Lockheed employee joins together the aft canopy or rear window of an early P-38 with a screwdriver, ratchet, and socket. Aircraft manufacturers employed thousands of women during the war. Even though they were generally labeled "Rosie, the Riveter," women often did a lot more than rivet, as seen here. *Lockheed Martin via Dennis Wrynn*

In comparison to the previous five years of testing, the dash seven moved quickly through the 150 hour Type Test program, which was run between 28 January 1937 and 23 March 1937. As the result, this engine was officially accepted 23 April 1937, making it the first USAAC powerplant to be qualified to operate at 1,000 bhp. As a follow-on, Allison was interested in obtaining certification for commercial use of this engine, and with USAAC approval, submitted the test results to the Department of Commerce for a Commercial Type Certificate. Allison was then issued Approved Engine Specification Number 177 for the V-1710C4 (commercial designation) on 13 July 1937.

The V-1710 Flies

Logically the USAAC wanted to see its new engine fly, and back in September 1936, they had issued their approval to construct the balance of the previously ordered service-test YV engines. This was based upon the progress then being made on

the testing of the dash seven engine. The first of these engines replaced the Curtiss-Wright V-1570 originally installed in a Consolidated A-11 (the non-supercharged version of the P-30/PB-2 aircraft). Sporting its new dash seven engine, the modified aircraft was redesignated A-11A. The modification work was accomplished by the newly organized Bell Aircraft Corporation. The first flight of the A-11A was made on 14 December 1936 and subsequently the airplane completed an extensive flight-test program to accumulate 300 hours—one complete engine-overhaul cycle. This was finalized with very few engine "squawks," and only minor parts, repairs, and replacements were required to rejuvenate the engine when finally overhauled. The A-11 airframe and V-1710 powerplant combination was then soon retired to Chanute Army Air Field, Illinois, where they became fixtures in the airframe and powerplant mechanic training programs for a number of years. (Interestingly, on the 28 March 1944 celebration of Allison's delivery of its 50,000th V-1710 engine, the USAAF returned "ole No. 9" to Allison for display.)

The remaining engines from the service-test hatch were used either for Type Test programs, or to power Curtiss XP-37 and Bell XFM-1 Airacuda aircraft. Allison also had underway a general V-1710 improvement program intended to provide an engine rated at 1,150 bhp. This was accomplished by improving several components and features of the powerplant, and at the same time, increasing the compression ratio from 6.00:1 to 6.65:1 to improve its overall efficiency. Another significant alteration, allowed by the previous improvements in the air intake manifold, was that the turbosupercharger gear ratio could be reduced from the type tested 8.00:1 to 6.23:1. This reduced the power required to drive the turbosupercharger while also lowering the temperatures in the induction system, further improving the efficiency of the engine. The new engine became known as the Allison V-1710C7 and was specified by the USAAC as the powerplant to be utilized in its 1937 twin- and single-engine pursuit-interceptor competitions, respectively under Circular proposals X-608 and X-609. These aircraft were required to have turbosupercharged V-1710C7 engines in order to achieve the specified performance requirement put forth by the USAAC.

Enter the XP-38

Numerous proposals were received from the major airframe contracting firms of the day in response to the pursuit-interceptor circulars. Two of these firms, new to pursuit aviation, were selected to build prototypes of their proposals.

Lockheed would build the twin-engine XP-38 and Bell would construct the single-engine XP-39.

As the XP-38 developed, a different engine model had to be defined for it since it was for a twin-engined airplane. The result was the Allison V-1710C8, which was otherwise similar to the V-1710C7. Both models were assigned the same military designation, V-1710-11.

About the same time the USAAC decided to procure thirteen service test Curtiss YP-37s and elected to power them with the V-1710-11 (C8). For this purpose, twenty engines (including seven spare engines) were ordered in late 1937. Having a higher priority, however, the first of these engines from this contract (Allison s/n 18) was delivered to Lockheed for its XP-38; number two was shipped to Curtiss for its YP-37 program. The balance of the order was primarily used by the proposed YP-37s, but delivered as V-1710-13s, or C10s. The difference being that the earlier float-type carburetors in the -11s, or C8s, were replaced by the then new Bendix Stromberg Pressure Carburetors.

Not only was the XP-38 a dual-engined airplane with a need to feather its propellers, the engines would have to rotate in opposite directions to cancel the torque effects of the propellers to greatly improve handling and comfort for the pilot.

Allison met this requirement by providing the left-hand rotating V-1710C9, military designation XV-1710-15. It was built from V-1710C8 components, but on a separate contract. Only one of these engines was built, known as Allison s/n 17. The reversal of rotation (now counterclockwise) was accomplished by providing an opposite-order crankshaft and simply revising the engine firing order, using an opposite-turning starter motor, and installing an idler gear in the accessories drive housing so that the magneto, distributors, cams, and turbosupercharger all spun in the same direction (clockwise) as before. Allison offered to provide this modification to any of the contracted V-1710C8 engines at $2,900 each, should the USAAC desire additional backward-running V-1710C9s. As an aside, during the Depression years the military received great values for its limited funds!

With the loss of the XP-38 on its simultaneous delivery and speed-record-attempt flight, and following the USAAC's order for thirteen service test YP-38s, an opportunity was created to incorporate a new engine then being proposed by Allison.

Also rated at 1,150 bhp, this new engine was to use components coming from the E series engine being developed for the Bell XP-39 under project X-609, along with a more conventional "external spur" reduction gear. The selected engine was the Allison V-1710F2, with its most notable difference being the higher centerline of the propeller shaft, along with close-coupling to the crankshaft and an improved accessories section. Gone was the streamlined nose case. These new engines were designed to provide both right-hand and left-hand turning propellers by the expedient of installing the symmetrical crankshafts end-for-end, rewiring the firing order, mounting an opposite-turning starter motor, and installing an idler gear in the accessories drive section.

With these powerplants the USAAC established the practice of assigning each handed engine its own model number, ergo the V-1710-27 (F2R) and V-1710-29 (F2L) for the YP-38 aircraft. These engines were used for all the early production Lockheed Lightnings and Photo Lightnings up to the P-38F and F-4.

Allison worked hard to keep the V-1710 engines in the P-38/F-4/F-5 aircraft up to the demands of combat, both with respect to reliability and power. Since the P-38 series of aircraft were turbosupercharged (except for the British-ordered P-322s), its engines operated at "sea level" ratings. This means that full takeoff power was available from sea level up to the critical altitude, as defined by the allowable speed of the extremely hot-running turbine wheels. Actual increases in performance of the various P-38 series aircraft were paced by the octane rating of the aviation gasoline available in the theaters of operation they attended, the gear ratio chosen for the internal engine-driven supercharger stage, and the degree of intercooling of the hot air coming from the turbo section: no "trick" hot rod antics such as boring and stroking were attempted by either Allison at home or maintenance depots in the field.

When the 8th Air Force of the USAAF began operations in England in 1942 it was quickly determined that maximum performance was critical to combat success, and that the British had an entirely different philosophy regarding the rating of combat aircraft engines. Whenever the British considered that an in-service engine was "reliable," it decided it was time to increase its peak power rating! Conversely, the U.S. War Department and USAAF took a more cautious approach focused on achieving maximum reliability and manufacturers guarantees. With the concurrence of 8th Air Force Headquarters, the 8th Air Force Technical Staff

NEXT PAGES
USAAC P-38Ds and RAF P-322s being constructed outside on 1 October 1941. Since the attack on Pearl Harbor was still a little more than two months off, no camouflage had been installed overhead as yet. Soon after December 7, this production area was hidden from the air. *Lockheed Martin via Dennis Wrynn*

began a systematic increase in authorized maximum power levels in combat Lightnings under its command in the fall of 1942. This was paced work done by Allison in Indianapolis during the summer of 1943, following which they provided recommended operating parameters for conditions that became known as War Emergency Rating or WER. In this way a combat pilot was provided with five minutes of peak power at quite high ratings without (hopefully) blowing up an engine. It took well over a year for the WER ratings to be officially sanctioned and supported by the War Department, though they were already in routine, if unofficial, use in combat theaters for some time.

As an airplane,specifically a pursuit-interceptor, the Lockheed XP-38 was truly ahead of its time. Though many may not be readily discernible, numerous unique features were incorporated in it and its subsequent offspring. Just one example in this regard is the aircraft's intercoolers. Any supercharger, acting as an air compressor, will significantly increase the temperature of the air passing through it. This is an unavoidable consequence of compression, and is further aggravated by the inefficiencies inherent in the actual machine doing the compression. In the P-38/F-4/F-5 series of aircraft, the turbosupercharger acted as a first-stage compressor, delivering heated sea level pressure to the engine carburetor. Since the turbosuperchargers were physically separated from the powerplants, space was available to install the intercoolers in front of the engine carburetors, and in this way the air intake manifold temperatures could be controlled. Everything in an aircraft is a compromise, and in this case the problem becomes the drag due to the need to bring cooling air onboard for the intercoolers. Lockheed's Kelly Johnson came up with a masterful solution of simply building the intercoolers into the leading-edge sections of the wings. Although the wing surface itself acted like a radiator in removing a portion of the unwanted heat, there was also a supply of cooling air taken from the slipstream and circulated through internal passages within the wing, where it picked up most of the heat and discharged it near the wingtips. As a result, the hot pressurized air coming from the turbos was cooled prior to delivery to the engine carburetors. This was indeed an elegant solution, and it provided a measure of anti-icing for the wing in the process!

This feature was designed to be adequate for the 1,150 bhp C series engines used in the early P-38s. When the higher power levels demanded for combat at WERs, or the heavily loaded take-offs for long-range escort missions were considered, the integral wing-mounted intercoolers were found to no longer be adequate. The solution was the "chin" installation of core-type intercoolers, installed directly below the engines between the oil coolers. The intercooler heat was then removed by air passing through the core and exiting through doors in the bottom of the engine nacelles. This configuration was introduced with the advent of the P-38J and proved to be perfectly adequate. The revised arrangement had the added advantage of making the leading-edge volume available for fuel, resulting in an additional 55 gallons available in each wing.

Over the long development and production life of the P-38/F-4/F-5 airplanes (1937-1945), the aircraft and its engines went through numerous evolutions and improvements. The result is that there are many different sources of performance data and listings of aircraft capabilities. Putting them all on an equal basis can be challenging, but the table below shows the ratings in effect when the particular model was the primary mission airplane. One WER not listed is that for the F series V-1710-111 and V-1710-113 engines in the P-38L, which some references give as 1,725 bhp at 3,000 rpm. The difference is that the rating is appropriate when the engine is run at 3200 rpm, which was never an authorized handbook rating during the war. The 150 Lockheed P-322 "Castrated Lightnings" built for the British came about because of the inability of the United States to provide enough of the critically needed turbosuperchargers to meet the demands of the twin-engined USAAF P-38s, not to mention the high priority four-engined Boeing B-17s and Consolidated B-24s. As a

Lockheed P-38/F-4/F-5 Production Engines

Variant	Engine/Dash Number	GE Turbo Model	Takeoff bhp*
XP-38	V-1710-11/-15 (C8/C9)	B-2	1,150
YP-38	V-1710-27/-29 (F2R/L)	B-2	1,150
P-38	V-1710 27/-29 (F2R/L)	B-2	1,150
P-38D	V-1710-27/-29 (F2R/L)	B-2	1,150
P-38E	V-1710-27/-29 (F2R/L)	B-2	1,150
F-4	V-1710-17/-29 (F2R/L)	B-2	1,150
P-38F	V-1710-49/-53 (F5R/L)	B-2	1,325
	V-1710-49/-53 (F5R/L)	B-2	1,325
P-38G	V-1710-51/-55 (F10R/L)	B-13	1,325
F-5A	V-1710-51/-55 (F10R/L)	B-13	1,325
P-38K	V-1710-75/-77 (FI5R/L)	B-14	1,425
P-38H-1	V-1710-89/-91 (F17R/L)	B-13	1,425
P-38H-5	V-1710-89/-91 (F17R/L)	B-33	1,415
P-38J	V-1710-89/-91 (F17R/L)	B-33	1,425
F-5B	V-1710-89/-91 (F17R/L)	B-33	1,425
P-38L	V-1710-111/-113 (F30R/L)	B-33	1,425
P-322	V-1710-33 (C15)	None	1,040

* All bhp ratings given with engines at 3000 rpm

A P-38F-1-LO (41-7586) in its natural element. This type was the first version of the Lightning to be declared combat ready. Powered by the 1,325 horsepower V-1710-49/-53 engines, it was capable of 413 mph at an altitude of 20,000 feet. *Lockheed Martin via Dave Ostrowski*

result, the P-322 Lightnings were built with the "altitude" rated C series V-1710-33s then being used in the Curtiss P-40 Tomahawks. The lighter weight, as the result of uninstalled turbos, was not enough to compensate for the lower rated engines. In addition, they were not "handed" engines; that is, left-turning engines were not available to the P-322s.

First flown by the USAAC in late 1936 with its original normal rating of 750 bhp, and a maximum takeoff rating of 1,000 bhp, the then non-super-charged V-1710 was the most powerful inline aircraft engine of the time. Consequently, it was also used to power production Bell P-39s, Curtiss P-40s, and Bell P-63s. By the end of the war, the Allison Engine Company Division of the General Motors Corporation had produced more than 80,000 V-1710 engines in a number of series and many dash numbers. All said and done, it was a hallmark engine that helped the United States and its allies win World War II.

CHAPTER THREE

FLYIN' HIGH: TURBOSUPERCHARGERS

The P-38/F-4/F-5 series of aircraft were powered by a pair of turbosupercharged engines that were critical to their outstanding performances at high altitude. Lightnings could use sea-level power ratings at high altitudes and thereby outperform their adversaries. Again, with passages from Dan Whitney's upcoming book, *Vees For Victory*, the excerpts as follows explain the development of supercharged aircraft engines.

Turbosupercharging the Allison V-1710 Aircraft Engine

Military tacticians in the 1930s were focusing on bombardment aircraft with turbosupercharged engines as a way to fly above the pursuit aircraft that they would likely encounter. Lieutenant Ben Kelsey, USAAC officer in charge of the Pursuit Aircraft Projects Office at Wright Field in 1935, believed that the next generation of pursuits would therefore need outstanding performance to be capable of intercepting such bombers. With this in mind he was instrumental in structuring the USAAC 1937 Interceptor Competition to develop and produce aircraft with the capacity to engage high-flying bombardment aircraft. While he would have liked to have a turbosupercharged 1,500 bhp engine for these aircraft, none were available. The most powerful engine then in existence was the aforementioned 1,150 bhp Allison V-1710C7, supercharged by the General Electric Model F-10 exhaust-driven turbosupercharger, which the USAAC had procured for this engine.

A major reason for the engine to have been interesting to the USAAC in the first place was its inherent ability to accept turbosupercharging. At

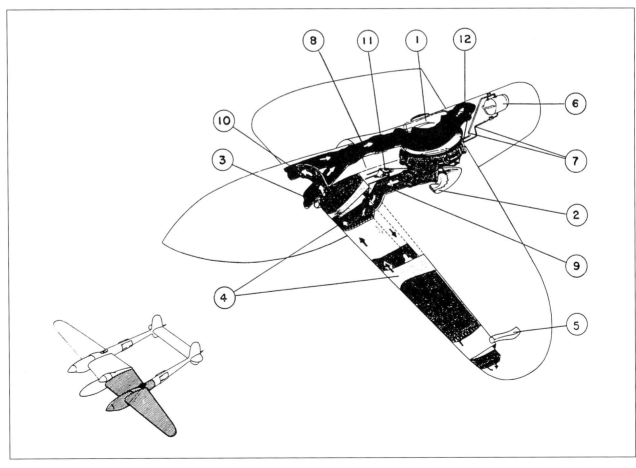

Turbosupercharger installation as on P-38D, E, F, G, and H versions of the Lightning. *USAF*

the time, limitations on the ability to air-cool large radial engines, coupled with the comparatively poor aviation fuels available, meant that only a liquid-cooled engine could take full advantage of the turbosupercharger, which the Air Service had been developing since 1918. It was this concept that directly led to the circular proposals X-608 and X-609 and the 1937 interceptor competitions, which in turn spawned the Lockheed XP-38 and the Bell XP-39.

Developing the Turbosupercharger

During World War I, Professor A.C.E. Rateau in France produced a gas turbine-driven supercharger that allowed aircraft to attain previously unheard-of altitudes. The U.S. Army Air Service brought the concept to the United States in 1918 intending to produce a similar, but improved indigenous device. It

1. Turbosupercharger
2. Carburetor air-intake scoop
3. Intercooler cooling-air-intake-scoop
4. Intercooler
5. Intercooler cooling-air discharge
6. Turbosupercharger oil-supply tank
7. Turbosupercharger oil-supply lines
8. Engine exhaust stack to nozzlebox inlet
9. Air-induction ducting from turbosupercharger to intercooler
10. Air-induction ducting from intercooler to carburetor
11. Turbosupercharger waste pipe

assigned the project to develop an exhaust-driven turbosupercharger to the Experimental Department of the Airplane Engineering Division at McCook Field, Dayton, Ohio. With cooperation from Dr. William F. Durand of the NACA (later NASA), who was aware of earlier work to develop a gas turbine engine for General Electric, the project went forward. Doctor Durand asked General Electric to detail Dr. Moss in the effort to develop a turbosupercharger suitable for use on aircraft. This request, in turn, led to a rapid development effort by Dr. Moss's team, who soon had a 400 bhp Liberty-12 engine operating successfully at the top of Pike's Peak, Colorado

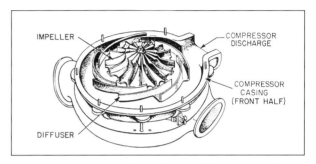

Centrifugal compressor section shown in the General Electric B-type turbosupercharger. *General Electric Aircraft Engines*

(14,110 feet above sea-level), as a location to demonstrate and investigate the effectiveness of their turbosupercharger. Following World War I a more measured development program was continued, with moderate funding by the U.S. Army for the next two decades. As a result General Electric produced a series of turbosuperchargers of steadily improving design and materials, leading to viable units being in-service with the USAAC at the beginning of World War II. These were the first examples of successful aviation-related gas turbine engines.

A supercharger can be used with an engine to do one, or both, of two functions. For an automotive engine a supercharger increases the quantity of air being processed by the engine, and since engine power is determined by the amount of air with which fuel can be mixed and combusted, the power can be increased to a level typical of a physically larger cubic-inch displacement engine. This of course assumes that the engine is strong enough to handle the increase in power without damage. The second way a supercharger can be used is to compensate for the lack of air available to an engine, such as what happens when an engine is being operated at high altitudes. In this case the power rating of the engine is not usually increased, rather the engine produces its maximum power up to the ceiling, as defined by the ability of the supercharger to deliver sea-level pressure air (14.7 pounds per square inch).

Superchargers themselves can appear in many forms, but all are simply one type or another of a mechanical compressor. Many types have been used, but for aircraft they need to be compact and light weight. One type that was used in some early between the eye and periphery, the periphery is traveling at a much higher tangential velocity. This velocity is imparted to the exiting air, often bringing it very close to the speed of sound (1,116.45 feet per second at sea-level in the standard atmosphere). High speed air itself is not terribly useful within the engine, so it is passed through a diffuser, which efficiently slows the air by changing its kinetic energy into pressure and heat. It is this high pressure, compressed air, which is then fed into the engine.

The degree of pressure increase (or boost) defines the minimum amount of power which will be required to compress the air. Much more power is required at high altitudes than at low or medium altitudes, due to the need for a greater relative pressure increase. This suggests that it is a good idea to vary the speed of the impeller so that the supercharger just provides the desired pressure and none of the power has to be wasted by

An actual Type B turbosupercharger is shown here in cutaway form. *General Electric Aircraft Engines*

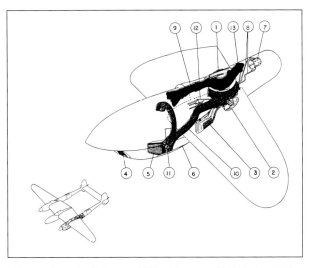

Turbosupercharger installation as on P-38J and K versions of the Lightning. *USAF*

attempts was the Roots Blower, but its mechanical complexity, close tolerances, weight, and inherently poor efficiency ruled it out as a desirable unit.

The nearly universal supercharger for use on reciprocating aircraft engines became the centrifugal-flow-type compressor (a compressor having one or more vaned rotary impellers which accelerate the incoming air radially outward into a diffuser, compressing by centrifugal force). This machine is nearly ideal in that it has only one moving part (the impeller) though it must rotate at comparatively high speeds to achieve the desired degree of compression. The physical process involves drawing outside air into the eye or center of the spinning impeller, where radially fixed blades then direct the air through a passage to the periphery. Due to the difference in radius

1. Turbosupercharger
2. Carburetor air-intake scoop
3. Air filter
4. Intercooler cooling-air-intake-scoop
5. Intercooler
6. Intercooler cooling-air discharge
7. Turbosupercharger oil-supply tank
8. Turbosupercharger oil-supply lines
9. Engine exhaust stack to nozzlebox inlet
10. Air-induction ducting from turbosupercharger to intercooler
11. Air-induction ducting from turbosupercharger to carburetor
12. Turbosupercharger regular
13. Turbosupercharger waste gate

Nearly new F-5F-6-LOs (derived from P-38L-5-LOs) sharing base space with B-24s, B-25s, C-47s, and PBY-4s. *Frank Carr via Jeff Ethell*

throttling the airflow. It is at this point that one of the true advantages of powering the supercharger with a turbine becomes apparent, for if properly sized, the turbine can be easily controlled to give exactly the correct speed or rpm to produce the desired airflow and pressure. A good reciprocating aircraft engine will usually discharge about half of the supplied fuel's energy in the form of high temperature exhaust gases leaving the cylinders. If these gasses can he put to work, the efficiency of the installation can be greatly improved. Running them through a turbine, and using the developed power to drive the supercharger, then becomes an advantageous way to utilize otherwise-lost power. Meeting the full requirements of the P-38 series of aircraft at their critical altitude of 25,000 feet required about 200 to 400 bhp to drive the supercharger (depending upon the demanded engine power, which was

proportional to airflow), while there was well over 700 bhp of recoverable horsepower in the exhaust gasses. With the large amount of waste energy available in the V-1710's exhaust gasses, there was little incentive to improve the component efficiencies of the compressor and turbine used in the exhaust-driven turbosupercharger. Each was typically in the range of 60 to 65 percent efficient. In comparison, new modern gas turbine engines used to power aircraft will have compressors that are 85 to 90 percent efficient and turbines with efficiencies in the low 90 percent range.

As a result of these comparatively low efficiencies, a large amount of extra heat was created in the supercharger, and it all showed up in temperatures that were too high for reliable operation of the engine. Fortunately, much of the aerial combat over Europe was in very cold and frigid temperatures at altitude. Such conditions provided a mea-

The Lightning was arguably the best all-around fighter of World War II. With a gross weight of 17,500 pounds in its final P-38L form, it was 3,000 pounds heavier than the Republic P-47D Thunderbolt, and 7,400 pounds heavier than the North American P-51D Mustang. Their respective maximum speeds were 414, 428, and 437. *Jeff Ethell Collection*

Once in the field (after many hours of U.S.-based school instructions) P-38 airframe and powerplant mechanics faced many technical order changes to keep their Lightnings up to USAAF standard. Here, an instructor gives some of them new methods of maintenance. *Jeff Ethell Collection*

This war-weary P-38H-5-LO (42-66948) has been stripped of its guns and cannon and awaits final disposition after the war. While most P-38s, F-4s, and F-5s were scrapped, some survived and are now in the hands of private owners and museums. *Dave Ostrowski Collection*

sure of safety when WER power levels were required by the early models of the P-38.

With the introduction of the P-38J and the P-38L models, a new intercooling system was provided. The engine nacelles were completely revised to incorporate core-type intercoolers. These provided the needed additional cooling capacity, while at the same time being controllable. This was an advantage, for having the induction air too cold created difficulties in getting the fuel to properly evaporate and provide uniform mixture to the cylinders.

Turbosupercharging the V-1710

In December 1932 the USAAC ordered their first version of the Allison V-1710, the XV-1710-1, which like all following U.S. Army V-1710s, incorporated a single-stage engine-driven supercharger. They required the engine to be designed to develop 1,000 bhp, and to be suitable for turbo-supercharging with the use of its exhaust gasses. One of the primary reasons for USAAC interest in the V-1710 was that as a liquid-cooled engine it would be more tolerant of turbosupercharging, and in this way give the USAAC a whole new capability with respect to altitude and power. On 31 January 1933 the Material Division at Wright Field requested the General Electric Company to adapt one of their turbosuperchargers to the V-1710, designing it to be able to deliver 1,000 bhp at up to 20,000 feet. General Electric immediately

went to work along lines suggested by Wright Field, who had wanted the new unit to be based on the General Electric Model F-2E unit, then in limited production for aircraft powered by the 600 bhp Curtiss-Wright V-1570 Conqueror engine. It soon discovered that a direct conversion of the existing F-2E model would not be viable, mainly because of the excessive amount of back pressure imposed upon the engine to achieve the demanded performance for an engine as large as the V-1710.

General Electric's solution was a new and larger unit, specifically sized for the V-1710. This unit was designated as the Model F-8, which evolved in 1935 to become the Model F-10 turbosupercharger. Like their earlier units, this unit used a single-stage compressor and a centrifugal impeller, a fixed diffuser, and was driven by a single-stage axial-flow (parallel to the rotor's axis of rotation) turbine.

General Electric's fifteen years of experience designing, building, and testing these units had taught them that the preferred design concept was to have the unit deliver its compressed air at a pressure sufficiently above sea-level to compensate for the friction of pumping the air through the intercooler and the pressurized carburetor. Separately, the exhaust turbine driving the supercharger impeller acts as an obstruction to the free-flow of exhaust gasses, and as a result causes back pressure on the engine. The effect of this back pressure is to cause the

An F-5E Photo Lightning of the 3rd PRG flies near its base in Florence, Italy, in late-1944. This is one of 100 P-38J-15-LOs that were created at Lockheed's modification facility in Dallas, Texas. *Mark Adamic Collection*

Izzy Levine at Nuthampsted, England in 1944. He poses with a P-38J of the 8th AF, 55th FG. *Mark Adamic Collection*

pistons to, in effect, pump (or push) the exhaust gasses out and to overcome the obstruction created by the turbine. Obviously, this reduces the power available to drive the propeller(s) and thus, it is unwanted. General Electric recommended that the turbine be sized so that the unwanted back pressure be no greater than the delivery pressure produced by the supercharger unit. In this fashion, the engine never realized it was not in operation at sea level! These were the reasons that they had to design a new, and physically larger, unit for the 1,000 bhp V-1710 engine. The resulting impeller was 12.25 inches in diameter, and the turbine 12 inches.

Turbosupercharging the V-1710 for the P-38

The physical arrangement of the P-38 accommodated the installation of turbosuperchargers quite nicely. By being located directly behind the engines, the exhaust collector manifolds were relatively short, with each bank of six cylinders being collected in groups of two, with a simple slip-sleeve joint to accommodate thermal (or heat) expansion between them. These were routed to a y-connector just behind and above the engine, which then led directly to the turbine manifold and nozzle box.

Control of the flow through the turbine was accomplished by the waste gate, installed on the aft end of the nozzle box. Combustion air was ducted from the slipstream via a scoop located in the high pressure airstream existing just below the wing, to the compressor inlet. The hot compressed air was then routed forward to the intercooler, and from there to the engine carburetor. A small scoop just ahead of the unit directed cooling air from the slipstream into the cooling cap and onto the red-hot turbine wheel.

By the time the one-of-a-kind XP-38 was prepared for its first flight-test in January 1939, General Electric had moved beyond its original Model F-10 turbosupercharger. While the dimensions of the important impeller and turbine units had not changed, they were configured differently. Furthermore, the USAAC had changed their nomenclature system for aircraft accessories, under which superchargers and turbosuperchargers were classified. Consequently the two turbosupercharger units installed on the XP-38s Allison V-1710-11/-15 (C8/C9) engines were now designated as the General Electric Type B-2 (see below).

For the new impeller and turbine configurations, General Electric had tailored the diffuser on the compressor, as well as the flow area of the

An F-5B of the 9th AF, 67th TRG, 33rd PRS at Charlerois, Belgium in October 1944. Converted from P-38J-1-LOs, 200 F-5B-1-LOs were built. *Mark Adamic Collection*

turbine nozzles, for the 1,150 bhp capability of the engines powering the XP-38. This became the method that General Electric used to match turbosuperchargers to many aircraft over the coming years, and it helps to explain the variety of Type B units. This family of turbos finally reached Model B-39, with all models believed to use impellers and turbine wheels with essentially the same dimensions.

The General Electric Type B Turbosupercharger

Successfully developed by the General Electric Company in the mid to late 1930s, the Type B turbosupercharger was a turbine-driven blower unit (also known as a supercharger) that was powered by the exhaust gases of its powerplant. In the case of the Lightning, there were two turbosuperchargers, one for each of the Allison V-1710s.

The improved Type B was first successfully tested all-out and in-flight on 5 July 1937 when Trans World Airlines's chief pilot D. W. Tomlinson captained a Northrop Gamma to 37,000 feet between Kansas City, Kansas, and Dayton, Ohio. That historic flight was the very first "over-the-weather" journey of an airplane between two distant cities.

Another concept imbedded into General Electric's scheme for sizing their turbos was that the Type Model prefix defined the range of horsepower for the engine for which the turbo would be intended to serve. These various Types would use the same rotating elements, with diffusers, nozzles, and ducting arrangements as required to adapt to specific installations (the Types being Type A, Type B, Type C, on through Type I) As developed, the major production models were Type Bs, which covered the range of 800 bhp to 1,400 bhp; the larger Type C units covered the range of 1,800 bhp to 2,200 bhp.

The design of the turbo was such that it could easily be configured to match the airframe specifics with respect to routing the various ducts and manifolds. The different configurations were known as Settings. This was accomplished by removing the tie bolts between the compressor and turbine casings and rotating them relative to each other. On the P-38/F-4/F-5 aircraft, Air Corps/Forces Setting Number 2, turbos were installed on the right-hand engine nacelle, and Setting Number 3 units on the left-hand nacelle. Although they were delivered from the factory both ways, the change was easily made in the field if an otherwise proper Type B unit was unavailable.

During its life the P-38/F-4/F-5 aircraft used several different engine models as well as different horsepower ratings—some requiring the turbos to support engine WERs as high as 1,725 bhp. How could this be accomplished with a turbo intended for operation on an engine rated at 1,400 bhp or less? As different operations were required, new and improved models of the basic Type B turbo were provided to match the engines, their ratings, and the missions of the aircraft.

As shown in the table below, three different turbosupercharger models were employed on the various production models of the Lightning aircraft. The Type B-2 was used for all the early models, up through the P-38F and some similarly powered P-38Gs and F-5As, which were powered by the same 1,325 bhp V-1710-49/-53 (F5R/L) engines. At this power level it was found to be a marginal performer and a new model was introduced, the Type B-13, which could only he used with the V-1710-51/-55 (F10R/L) engines. The significant difference between the Type B-13 and the Type B-2 was a new diffuser tailored for operation at 1,325 bhp. It was used on the P-38G and P-38H aircraft with their 1,325 bhp and 1,425 bhp engines respectively.

GE Turbosuperchargers Used by P-38/F-4/F-5 Aircraft

GE Turbo Model	Air Flow lb/min	rpm Speed @ Altitude
B-2	120	21,300
B-13	130	21,300
B-33	165	24,000

The P-38H—powered by the V-1710-89/-91 (F17R/L)—was rated for 1.425 bhp up to its critical altitude of about 25,000 feet. Because of intercooler limitations, the WER of 1,600 bhp from this engine could not be used, nor could the Type B-13 adequately support the WER. These limitations were both removed on the P-38J and P-38L models with their use of core-type or chin-mounted intercooler units, which were fed by improved Type B-33 turbosuperchargers.

The Type B-33 turbosupercharger used the same compressor as the Type B-13, but its turbine wheel and buckets were made of improved materials. These new materials allowed the turbine to turn at a higher rpm, which had the effect of increasing the critical altitude of the installation at a given power, or conversely, allowing higher power at lower altitudes. In this way the true capability of the engine could be utilized. In addition, a five-minute overspeed was allowed, but to be used only during WER conditions. The Type B-33s could be used in place of B-13s, but only in pairs, as they were not to be mixed on the same airplane.

Operations

The major problem with the operations of the Type B series of turbosuperchargers on P-38s was to properly control their speeds, and thereby their powerplant's manifold pressure settings.

This F-5G (44-26422) of the 41st PRS was based at Northwest Field, Guam, when VJ Day came about. In the background is a Boeing B-29 Superfortress of the 509th Bombardment Squadron, 351st Bombardment Group. They delivered the two atomic bombs—*Little Boy* and *Fat Man*—to Hiroshima and Nagasaki to end the war in the Pacific. *Mark Adamic Collection*

A P-38J named *Anet* of the 20th FG, 55th FS at Kings Cliffe, England, runs up both engines after maintenance. *Dave Ostrowski Collection*

Control was fundamentally easy, accomplished by simply opening or closing the waste gate and thereby controlling the amount of exhaust gases actually passing through the turbine. In this way the speed and power to the compressor could be accurately controlled. Since this would be a full time job for the pilot during combat, an automatic turbosupercharger controller was provided. The idea was that the pilot only had to set the desired engine speed (as controlled by the constant-speed propellers) and manifold pressure, usually with the engine throttles wide-open. The automatic control unit would then adjust the waste gate so that the turbos would maintain the set manifold pressure.

According to Lockheed engineering test pilot Tony LeVier, the proper way for a combat pilot to manage his engines was: "Whenever possible on combat missions, cruise at a low rpm with a high boost. This gives you maximum fuel economy and helps maintain a more desirable carburetor air temperature. Should you be jumped, your turbos will already be putting out and you have only to increase [engine] rpm to get your desired power."

Many of the early P-38s had tachometers linked to their turbosuperchargers. These were to

One important role for the P-38 was as a long-range bomber escort. It is here that its turbos became especially beneficial. In this regard it is constructive to compare the escort version of the North American P-51D Mustang and its two-stage Packard V-1650-7 Merlin engine, to the escort Lockheed P-38J/L aircraft. We will assume that these aircraft are in the long-range economy cruise configuration, without external fuel tanks.

The P-51D, which developed 520 bhp at 2000 rpm and a manifold pressure of 27 inches, when cruising at 16,500 feet, consumed 0.60 pounds per horsepower per hour. By comparison, the V-1710-111/-113 engines in the P-38L, cruising at 525 bhp each at 1600 rpm each at 15,000 feet and using a manifold pressure of 31 inches, consumed 0.46 pounds of fuel per horsepower per hour. The conditions are not quite the same, but close enough to see that the Packard-built Merlin required more fuel simply to drive its two-stage supercharger, even when the engine was throttled back, and in low gear.

The differences between the two types of aircraft are entirely due to the P-38s turbos providing the bulk of the power required to supercharge the engines at these altitudes. The effect would be greater above 20,000 feet, where the Merlin had to shift its superchargers into high gear. Had the P-38 been powered by a pair of the two-stage Merlins, as has been often suggested (and even studied by Lockheed during the war), the result would have been a decidedly short-legged P-38! Now proved, the economical cruise fuel–consumption rate of the two-stage Merlin—compared to the turbosupercharged V-1710-111/-113—is 30 percent higher!

The P-38s used three different models of the General Electric B series of turbosuperchargers: the B-2, capable of 21300 rpm; the B-13, capable of 21300 rpm; and the B-33, capable of 24000 rpm. Each type had a unit weight of 135 pounds; thus, their weight penalty was nearly non-existent compared to their importance.

Without any doubt, today's war babies for the most part—those born during the 1941–45 time period, do not fully realize just how important the capability was for U.S. aircraft to operate at such high altitudes (30,000 to 40,000 feet) during World War II. A large number of U.S. aerial victories are directly attributed to the use of evolving supercharger technologies. If not for the determined engineers at General Electric and Wright Field, and the availability of relatively new superchargers, the outcome of that war might have been very different. For not only did the advent of the supercharger allow the Lightning to be successful, it allowed high-flying bombers like the B-17 to better survive. Indeed, the supercharger was a significant part of U.S. victories over Europe and Japan.

tell the pilot the exact speed of the turbos, and let him know when he was at the critical or limiting turbo rpm. With the move to electronic turbo controls these were replaced by indicator lights in the cockpit that first flickered, then glowed red when the turbos reached their limiting/critical rpm. The tachometers then only fed the controlling circuits.

Maintenance of any type of airplane is critical to its performance, and one task unique to the Lightning was the rigging of the turbo controls so that they would be providing the same boost and so that the controls themselves would be working in concert.

This is a rare photo of a P-38J Droop Snoot Lightning at its base at Vincenzo Airfield, Italy. It belonged to the 82nd FG, 96th FS, and could carry a single 165 gallon drop tank and three 500 pound bombs. *Dave Ostrowski Collection*

An early F-5A of the 8th PRG in India. The F-5As featured more horsepower and better cameras than the earlier F-4s. Still, due to the constant improvements being made, only 180 F-5As were produced before even newer versions became available. *Dave Ostrowski Collection*

CHAPTER FOUR

EVOLUTION: P-38, F-4, AND F-5 VARIANTS

With any heavily produced series of aircraft, a large number of variants and sub-variants are designed, developed and built. And with eighteen distinct variants and numerous sub-variants, it was no different for the P-38, F-4, and F-5 series of aircraft. And in the end, with 10,038 Lightnings produced, Lockheed had established itself as a successful manufacturer of fighter-type aircraft. The evolution of the P-38 is as follows:.

Variants and Sub-Variants
The XP-38
Lockheed Model 22-64-01

Powered by a pair of 1,150hp Allison V-12 engines of 1,710cid each, spinning three-bladed inward-turning propellers, the short-lived XP-38 was able to attain a top speed of 413 mph at

Artist concept of the proposed but never produced P-38 Sea Lightning. Lockheed Martin

20,000 feet before its demise on 11 February 1939. Having just made its maiden test flight only fifteen days earlier, the first and only XP-38 airplane was good enough to not only establish an unofficial transcontinental speed record but to set the stage for the manufacture of 10,037 additional P-38 types. Due to its short life the XP-38 was never armed. However, for later tests, it had been scheduled to be armed with one 20mm cannon (with sixty rounds of ammunition), and four .50 calibre machine guns with 210 rounds per gun (rpg). Even though the XP-38 had died an early death, the USAAC was most impressed with its performance. And on 27 April 1939, two and a half months after the XP-38 had crashed, it ordered a single structural test airframe and thirteen service test YP-38s for the sum of $2 million.

The YP-38
Lockheed Model 122-62-02

For gun-firing trials, the YP-38s were armed with a single 37mm cannon (15 rounds), two .30 calibre machine guns with 500 rpg, and two .50 calibre machine guns with 210 rpg. The YP-38s were also used for wind-tunnel evaluations, cold climate tests, maintenance training, flight-test activities, and so on. Unlike the XP—which featured the Allison C-series V-1710, the YP's came with the improved F-series V-1710 engines. In their case, as with all other subsequent Lightnings, the YPs three-bladed propellers spinned outward instead of inward. With its V-1710-27/-29 engines, the YP-38's top speed was 405 mph at 20,000 feet. Moreover, and better than the USAAC had specified, they had a 3,333 feet per minute rate of climb. For Lockheed had something to prove: on 20 September 1939, long before the first YP-38 flew, the USAAC ordered sixty-six P-38s. And on 30 August 1940, eighteen days before the YP's first flight, it ordered another 410 aircraft. Highly rare and showing tremendous faith in an unproved airplane, the Air Corps had gambled to make Lockheed's day. With the very early demise of the XP-38 after only about twelve hours flying time, and with the still-to-be-evaluated YPs, Lockheed had already been guaranteed its new fighter's future with a 476–plane order in hand, starting with twenty-nine P-38-LOs (L-Lockheed, O-Burbank). The first example, with Lockheed test pilot Marshall Headle seated, made its first flight on 17 September 1940 at Lockheed Air Terminal, Burbank, California.

The P-38-LO
Lockheed Model 221-61-01

Powered by the same two engines used on the YP-38s, and likewise incorporating the same General Electric Model B-2 exhaust-driven turbosuperchargers as the XP and the YPs, the twenty-nine P-38-LOs included a 37mm cannon and four .50 calibre machine guns. Most of these were delivered to and accepted by the 1st FG located at Selfridge Field near Mount Clemens, Michigan, the first air corps fighter group to evaluate the YP-38s. Thus, it was qualified to receive the first production batch of P-38s. One P-38-LO, in fact the very first one

built (S/N 40-744), was delivered to Wright Field and modified for studies of the effects on pilots in a cockpit located outside of a plane's centerline. Since this batch of Lightnings were very-early production examples with no armor plating or other standard combat aircraft features, they were redesignated RP-38-LOs (R-restricted) as they were not capable of combat. Another P-38-LO was also used for special test purposes and is discussed below.

The XP-38A
Lockheed Model 622-62-10

Under USAAC Secret Project MX-6, a P-38-LO (S/N 40-762) was modified to test a type of pressurized cockpit in hope of adding such pilot accommodation in the future. Lockheed appointed Carl Haddon as XP-38A project engineer, and without armament (to save weight), the XP-38A began manufacturer's flight-test trials in May 1942, with Lockheed test pilot Joe Towel in control. Though no P-38 aircraft ever got pressurized cockpits, the XP-38A tests were successful.

Respectively, in October and November 1939, Lockheed had proposed two additional variants of the Lightning with the temporary but never applied designations of P-38B-LO and P-38C-LO. It remains unclear as to why these two proposed versions were never proceeded with. No P-38A-LOs were ordered or produced. Instead, subsequent Lightning models began with the D suffix. So, unlike most production runs of successful aircraft types, the Lightning clan did not have any A, B, and C production variants.

The P-38D-LO
Lockheed Model 222-62-08

Still not capable of combat, and later redesigned RP-38D, this version of the Lightning (thirty-five built) sported the same engines and armament as the P-38-LOs. Featuring self-sealing fuel tanks, a low-pressure oxygen system, and a retractable landing light, P-38Ds—redesignated RP-38Ds—were mostly used as combat training aircraft. Because of

NEXT PAGES
General arrangement drawing of similar P-38J and P-38L types. *Lockheed Martin*

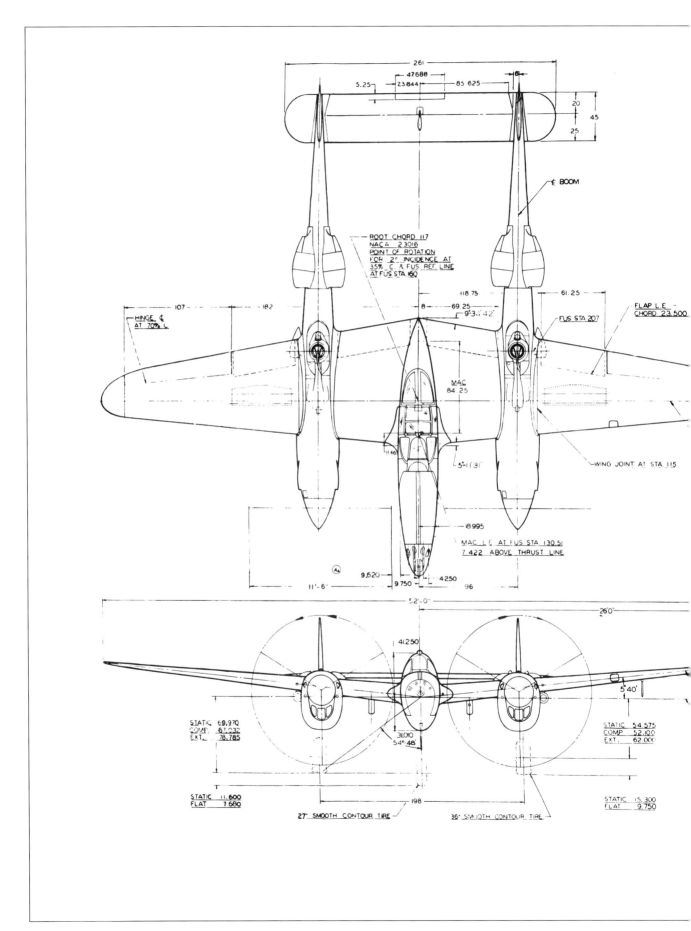

261
47.688
23.844
85.625
6
5.25
20
45
25
℄ BOOM

ROOT CHORD 117
NACA 23016
POINT OF ROTATION
FOR 2° INCIDENCE AT
35% C & FUS. REF. LINE
AT FUS STA 160

107
182
HINGE ℄
AT 70% C
118.75
61.25
8
69.25
9°-3'-42"
FUS STA 207
FLAP L.E
CHORD 23.500

MAC
84.25

11.46
5°-11'-31"
WING JOINT AT STA 115

18.995

MAC L.E AT FUS STA 130.51
7.422 ABOVE THRUST LINE

11'-6"
9.620
9.750
4.250
96
Ⓐ₄

52'-0"
26'0"
41.250
5° 40'

STATIC 69.970
COMP 67.032
EXT. 78.785

31.010
54° 48'

STATIC 54.575
COMP 52.100
EXT. 62.000

STATIC 11.600
FLAT 7.680

198

STATIC 15.300
FLAT 9.750

27" SMOOTH CONTOUR TIRE
36" SMOOTH CONTOUR TIRE

AREAS - % OF WING AREA -

HORIZONTAL TAIL SURFACES -	23.98
VERTICAL TAIL SURFACES -	14.91

TAB AREAS - SQ. FT -

ELEVATOR TAB	1.73
RUDDER TABS - TOTAL -	2.74

AREAS - SQ. FT. -

WING - PROJECTED PLANFORM		327.50
AILERONS	25.44	
HORIZONTAL TAIL SURFACES		78.54
STABILIZER	53.99	
ELEVATOR	24.55	
VERTICAL TAIL SURFACES		48.78
FINS	27.42	
RUDDERS	21.36	

SURFACE MOVEMENTS — DEGREES —

AILERON		
UP		25°
DOWN		20°
ELEVATOR		
UP		23°
DOWN		8½°
TAB - EACH WAY -	25°	
RUDDERS - EACH WAY -		28°
TABS - EACH WAY -	25°	

41.971
THEOR. TIP C.
NACA 4412
SEE NOTE

BEAM AT
RAIGHT LINE

(A₁)

CONDITION		MODEL (SERIAL)	
		P38J (4563)	P38L (4773)
GRO'S WEIGHT		15.916	16.195
EMPTY		13.260	13.539
NORMAL USEFUL LOAD		2.656	2.656
C.G. GROSS WT. GEAR UP.	DIM A	35.71	35.06
	DIM B	6.40	6.60
C.G. GROSS WT. GEAR DOWN	DIM A	33.38	32.75
	DIM B	4.10	4.30
C.G. FURTHEST FWD. LOADING	DIM A	31.87	31.57
	DIM B	4.20	4.20
C.G. FURTHEST AFT LOADING	DIM A	38.56	38.25
	DIM B	6.00	6.00
ANGLE α - GROSS WT. GEAR DOWN		16°18'	16°42'

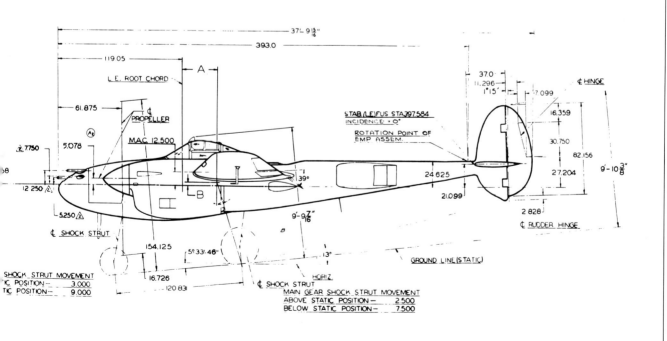

SHOCK STRUT MOVEMENT
TIC POSITION - 3.000
TIC POSITION - 9.000

MAIN GEAR SHOCK STRUT MOVEMENT
ABOVE STATIC POSITION - 2.500
BELOW STATIC POSITION - 7.500

THE WING SURFACE ARE SHOWN
NCE AND ARE MEASURED
LSS OTHERWISE NOTED
LE IS MEASURED AT THE BASIC CHORD
INCLUDE INCIDENCE THE WING IS BUILT
ND THEN ROTATED ABOUT THE INTER-
HE ℄ MAIN BEAM AND THE WING CHORD
HE SHIP UNTIL DESIRED INCIDENCE

6. WING STATIONS ARE MEASURED HORIZONTALLY
5. WING RIBS ARE SET VERTICALLY
4. BASIC MOLD LINE DRAWINGS SHOULD BE REFERRED TO
   FOR INFORMATION ON ORDINATES, CONTOURS, MASTER
   LOCATING DIMENSIONS, ETC. WHICH ARE NOT SHOWN ON
   THIS DRAWING OR DRAWINGS REFERENCED
3. BASIC NACA 4412 CHORD LINE LOCATED AT NEGATIVE 2° TO
   BASIC CHORD PLANE PASSING THROUGH NACA 23016
   CHORD LINE AT ROOT

⚠ VERTICAL DIMENSIONS TO GUNS ARE
TO ℄ GUNS AT FRONT TRUNNIONS.
1. ALL DIMENSIONS REFERRING TO
   EMP. VERTICAL SURFACES ONLY ARE
   ROTATED 1°15' COUNTER CLOCKWISE
   OF VERTICAL & HORIZ. RESPECTIVELY.
   NOTE -

the thicker-walled and heavier bullet-proof fuel cells, maximum internal fuel capacity had been reduced to 300 gallons (its predecessors could carry 410 gallons). The P-38Ds were obtained by the aforementioned 1st FG, and by the 14th FG at Hamilton Field, California, beginning in July 1941.

The P-38E-LO
Lockheed Model 222-62-09

Counting the one XP-38, 13 YP-38s, 29 P-38LOs, and 65 P-38D-L0s, the total number of Lightnings built was a mere 108 when production of the P-38E-LO began. But this model, with 210 examples on order, became Lockheed's first major production variant. Even with its improved electrical and hydraulic fluid systems, better flying instrumentation and adoption of a 20mm cannon with 150 rounds ammunition instead of a 37mm cannon with only fifteen rounds, the E model was still not thought of as a dedicated combat airplane. Still powered by the same engines as its YP-38, P-38-LO, and P-38D-LO predecessors, a large number of these aircraft were redesignated RP-38D and relegated to combat training and/or service test duties. But some P-38Es, working in concert with an undocumented number of P-38Ds, did see combat duties beginning in June 1942 following the Japanese invasion of Kiska and Attu in Alaska.

One P-38D (S/N 41-2048) was modified as a two-seater in 1942. This plane, featuring a lengthened center nacelle that projected aft of the wing trailing-edge, was used as a research vehicle to investigate the reduction of parasite drag on aircraft. And, as it turned out, it was the only Lightning to ever be fitted with dual flight controls.

The P-38F
Lockheed Model 222-60-09, the P-38F-LO; Model 222-60-15, the P-38F-1-LO; Model 222-60-12, the P-38F-5-LO; and Model 322-60-19, the P-38F-13-LO and P-38F-15-LO: These P-38s, produced in five blocks, totaled 377 aircraft and are discussed in order:

P-38F-LO
The 128 P-38F-LOs were the first Lightnings classified as combat-capable from the start. Powered by 1,325 horsepower Allison V-1710-49/-53 engines and armed the same as P-38Es, the F was capable of 395 mph at 25,000 feet.

P-38F-1-LO
With the same powerplant and armament as the above, the 149 P-38F-1-LOs featured underwing mounts (between the booms and fuselage) for

either two 1,000-pound bombs or two 165 gallon drop tanks; these capabilities were created from field modifications after their deliveries.

P-38F-5-LO
Powered and armed as above, Lockheed produced 100 P-38F-5-LO Lightnings. But this time their underwing mounts were factory-installed.

P-38F-13-LO & P-38F-15-LO
Respectively, these 29 -13-LOs and 111 -15-LOs were ordered by Great Britain through a cancelled French contract and were designated P-322s and named Lightning Is. Unhappy with their performance due to their lack of turbosupercharging (only 357 mph at 15,000 feet), the British did not accept them. The result was that the USAAF took over and procured them and ultimately they were brought up to Air Force standard. The -15-L0s unlike the -13-LOs had maneuvering flaps with an eight-degrees setting that allowed a tighter turning circle. These too were powered and armed like the aforementioned F models.

The P-38G
Lockheed Model 222-68-12, the P-38G-1-LO: Model 222-68-??, the P-38G-3-LO; Model 222-68-??, the P-38G-5-LO; Model 222-68-??, the P-38G-10-LO; Model 222-68-19, the P-38G-13-LO; and Model 222-68-??, the P-38G-15-LO: These P-38s, built in six blocks totaling 1,282 aircraft are discussed below.

P-38G-1-LO
Much like the P-38F-15-LOs but powered with 1,325hp V-1710-C· 51/-55 engines. Lockheed built 80 P-38-G-1-LO Lightnings. These first G models featured an improved radio and oxygen system.

P-38G-3-LO
Only twelve -3-LOs were built and their only difference from the above was that they came with GE B-13 turbosuperchargers in place of the B-2 units.

P-38G-5-LO
With only a better instrumentation package, sixty-eight 5-LOs were produced. A single -5-LO (S/N 42-12866) was used as an armament test plane for the XP-49; that is, it was fitted with four .50cal machine guns and two 20mm cannons.

P-38G-10-LO
Capable of carrying twelve 4.5in rockets in four three-tube launchers, or two 1,600lb bombs, or two 165gal drop tanks at underwing stores stations, 548 P-38G-10-LOs were built;

As three other P-38Es follow in single-file, an E model shows the location of its two GE B-2 turbosuperchargers and other close-up details. These four Es were assigned to the 82nd FG. *Lockheed Martin*

these also came with special equipment for operations in colder climates such as northern England and Alaska.

P-38G-13-LO

Very similar to the -3-LOs above, Lockheed manufactured 174 P-38G-13-LOs.

P-38G-15-LO

Lockheed built 200 P-38G-15-LOs, which were similar to the -5LOs. These were first ordered by the British Royal Air Force as Lightning IIs but instead were built for and used by USAAF units.

The P-38H-1-LO and P-38H-5-LO

Lockheed Model 222-81-20

Powered with 1,425hp V-1710-89/-91 engines, 226 P-38H-1-LOs were built. These P-38s. to allow the use of military power above 25,000 feet without overheating their engines, came with automated oil radiator cooling flaps; military power rose to 1,240hp from 1,150hp. Lockheed built 375 P-38H-5-LOs fitted with GE B-33 turbosuperchargers.

The P-38J

Lockheed Model 422

Beginning with ten service test (no Y prefix)

During construction one early production P-38 was set aside for modification into what was designated the XP-49. To answer USAAC CP 39-775, calling for an advanced interceptor pursuit airplane, Lockheed offered their Model 522. This XP-49 (S/N 40-3055), following brief flight-test activities, was scrapped in 1946 at Wright-Patterson AFB, Dayton, Ohio. Featuring a pressurized cockpit—as had been tested on a P-38 under USAAC Project MX- 6—the XP-49 was a close relative to its younger P-38 sibling. *Lockheed Martin*

model 422-81-14s designated P-38J-1-LO, another 1,000 J models would be produced in five more blocks as discussed below:

P-38J-5-LO

Like the above, these 210 -5-LOs featured many improvements which included a chin-type air inlet for the intercooler as had been tested on a P-38E (S/N 41-1983). And they were fitted with optimized air scoops on the booms for the Prestone coolant.

P-38J-10-LO

Featuring flat panel windscreens on their cockpit canopies, 790 P-38J-10-LOs came off the Burbank assembly lines. Like the J models above, and in fact like the P-38H-5-LOs, these were powered with V-1710-89/-91 engines driving General Electric B-33 turbosuperchargers.

P-38J-15-LO and P-38J-20-LO

These model 422-81-22s—respectively 1,400 J-15s and 350 J-20s—came equipped with a new electrical system and improved turbosupercharger governors. A pair of -20s (S/Ns 44-23544 and 44-23549) were field modified during the fall of 1944 to serve as single-place night fighter prototypes. Modified in Australia with Army-Navy AN/APS-4 radar units in a pod under their right wings, these were evaluated under combat conditions in the Philippines and New Guinea. Some J models, modified in the field as tandem-seat piggyback trainers, were called TP-38J-LOs. Carrying the AN/APS-4 radar unit, some of these were used to train P-38M Night Lightning pilots and radar operators. And a number of P-38Js—with glazed nose enclosures instead of forward-firing armament—were equipped with either the Bombing Through Overcast (BTO) bombardment radar or a Norden bomb sight and operated by bombardiers: these were known as *Droop Snoot* Lightnings.

P-38J-25-LO
Lockheed Model 422-81-23

210 P-38J-25s were built with electrically-driven dive flaps and hydraulically-boosted and powered ailerons.

The P-38K-LO
Lockheed Model 422-85-14

One of these was created using a P-38G-10-LO airplane (S/N 42-13558). Powered with 1,425 horsepower V-1710-75/-77 engines

Another Lightning-derived Lockheed bird was its husky big sibling—an experimental bomber escort and anti-shipping plane, the Model 20 (temporary design number L-134) Chain Lightning. Powered by two 2,600 horsepower turbosupercharged 24 cylinder liquid-cooled Allison V-3420-11/-13 engines, Lockheed's Joe Towel completed its first flight on D-Day (6 June 1944). A second XP-58 (S/N 41-2671) was canceled before its manufacture. *Lockheed Martin*

spinning wider-chord three-bladed propellers, the one-of-a-kind K model had J model-type nacelles and booms, and was the only one to use the GE model B-14 turbosupercharger.

The P-38L

Respectively, Lockheed produced 1,290 P-38L-1-LOs and some P-38L-5-LOs. Powered by V-1710-111/-113 engines driving GE B-33 turbosuperchargers, these were the last production models of the Lightning fighter series.

The P-38L-l-LO

Except for their 1,475 horsepower engines, these were much like the P-38J-25s, and as TP-38L-1-LOs. Some were modified and used as trainer aircraft.

The P-38L-5-LOs

These aircraft were capable of Droop Snoot operations and carried, among other ordnance, ten five-inch unguided rockets each under either outer wing panel. And they could carry either two 300 gallon external drop-type fuel tanks or two 2,000-pound bombs. Due to VJ Day, most of these were never finished; 2,520 had been ordered.

The P-38L-5-VN

To be built by Consolidated-Vultee Aircraft Corporation at its Nashville, Tennessee, plant, the USAAF ordered 2,000 P-38L-5-VNs similar to Lockheed-built P-38L-5-LOs. But again due to VJ Day, most of these were never built. In the end, only 113 were actually produced.

The P-38M Night Lightning

Being 37 mph faster than the Northrop P-61A Black Widow, the Lockheed P-38M Night Lightning served as a dedicated radar-equipped and rocket-, machine gun, and cannon-armed nighttime fighter. Painted overall gloss black, these good-looking two-place aircraft were not produced on the Burbank production line. Instead, using 75 P-38L-5s, Lockheed's modification center in Dallas, Texas, made the conversions. A P-38L-5-LO (S/N 44-25237) served as the type's basis. Fitted with the AN/APS-6 radar unit in an undernose pod and flash-suppressing

NEXT PAGES
Cutaway drawing of P-38 Lightning. *Lockheed Martin via Dennis Wrynn Collection*

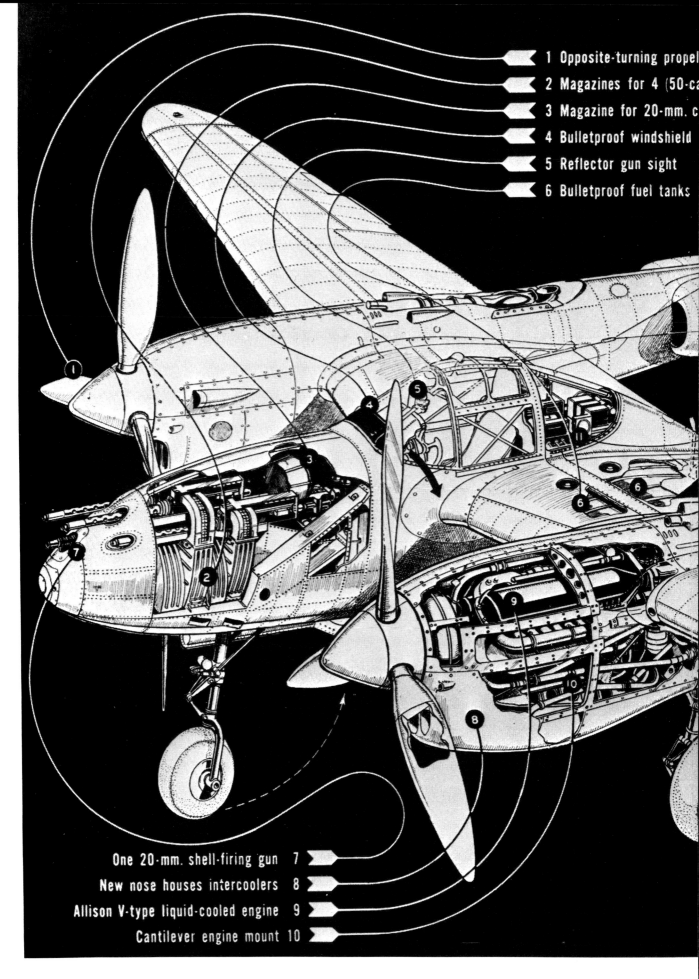

1 Opposite-turning propel[ler]
2 Magazines for 4 (50-ca[l]
3 Magazine for 20-mm. c[annon]
4 Bulletproof windshield
5 Reflector gun sight
6 Bulletproof fuel tanks

One 20-mm. shell-firing gun 7
New nose houses intercoolers 8
Allison V-type liquid-cooled engine 9
Cantilever engine mount 10

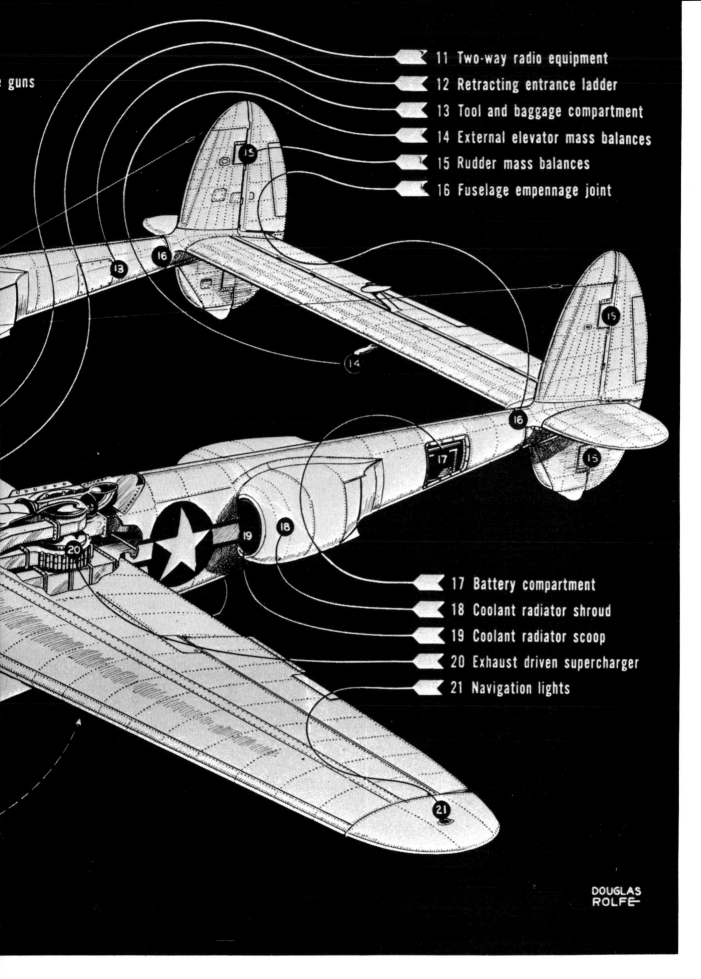

e guns

11 Two-way radio equipment
12 Retracting entrance ladder
13 Tool and baggage compartment
14 External elevator mass balances
15 Rudder mass balances
16 Fuselage empennage joint

17 Battery compartment
18 Coolant radiator shroud
19 Coolant radiator scoop
20 Exhaust driven supercharger
21 Navigation lights

DOUGLAS
ROLFE

This P-38L-5-LO (S/N 44-25419) is on a manufacturer's test hop over southern California. Late model Lightnings such as this one were finished in natural aluminum and featured the new national markings for military aircraft. *Lockheed Martin*

gun/cannon muzzles, the P-38Ms had a top speed of 406 mph at 15,000 feet. They did not see much in the way of combat action, however, as they were just entering service when VJ Day came about.

The F-4 Series
The F-4-1-LO
Lockheed Model 222-62-13

For high-speed photographic reconnaissance and mapping missions, the F-4 Photo Lightning was developed. Originally procured as P-38E fighters and powered by V-1710-21/-29 engines, these 99 former E models were completed as unarmed F-4s carrying four K-17 cameras in their noses. Used mostly for training and given the R for restricted prefix, these aircraft were later designated as RF-4-1-LOs.

The F-4A-1-LO
Lockheed Model 222-60-13

Armed with four K-17 cameras as the above, and powered with the 1,325 horsepower V-1710-49/-53 engines, Lockheed produced 20

F-4A-1-LOs. These were created from P-38F-1-LO airframes. The four K-17 cameras used by this and the previous version of the F-4/F-4A had six-inch focal lengths and were capable of both vertical (down-looking) and oblique (side-looking) photography; these were called trimetrogon units.

The F-5
The F-5A-2-LO
Lockheed Model 222-62-16

This one-of-a-kind Photo Lightning was a converted P-38E (S/N 41-2157), powered by 1,150 horsepower V-1710-21/-29 engines; it served as the prototype for the F-5A series.

The F-5A-1-LO, F-5A-3-LO, and F-5A-10-LO
Lockheed Model 222-68-16

Respectively, modified from P-38G airframes, Lockheed produced 20 -1-LOs, 20 -3-LOs, and 140 -10-LOs. These were all powered by V-1710-51/-55 engines of 1,325 horsepower. These Photo Lightnings carried five cameras: four K-17s and one K-24.

A posing P-38J-5-LO Lightning and an F-5B-1-LO Photo Lightning show the differences and similarities in their overall configurations. While the P-38J was armed, the F-5B was unarmed, yet both were powered with the same 1,425 horsepower V-1710-89/-91 engines. The F-5B's camera bag held two six-inch K-17 oblique units, a 12- or 24-inch K-17 vertical unit, and a 24-inch X-18 vertical unit. *Lockheed Martin*

The F-5B-1-LO
Lockheed Model 422-81-21

Using the P-38J-5-LO airframe and powerplant combination (V-1710-89/-91), 200 F-5B-1-LOs were manufactured by Lockheed at Burbank. These aircraft carried the same camera array as the earlier F-5A-10-LOs.

The F-5C

Using P-38J airframes at its modification center at Dallas, Texas, Lockheed created as many as 123 F-5C-1-LOs. These were for the most identical to the F-5B-1-LO aircraft that had also been modified from J model Lightning fighters.

The XF-5D

This one-of-a-kind Photo Lightning testbed airplane was the prototype of a proposed two-seater to be armed with two nose-mounted .50 calibre machine guns and three K-17 cameras (one in its nose and one in either tail boom). Modified from an F-5A-10-LO (S/N 42-12975), the camera man was stationed in the nose of the plane behind a glazed nose a la Droop Snoot types. The type was never produced.

The F-5E

Three versions of the F-5E became the F-5E-I-LO, F-5E-3-LO, and F-5E-4-LO. The 100 -2-LOs were created from P-38J-15-LOs; the 105 -3-LOs were from P-38J-25-LOs; and the 500 -4LOs were modified P-38L-1-LO aircraft. Using K-17 and K-18 cameras for the most part, the Photo Lightnings were similar to the earlier F-5C-1-LOs.

The F-5F

A prototype F-5F was created from an F-5B-I-LO (S/N 42-68220) and featured a different camera arrangement for service F-5F-3-LOs based on P-38L-5-LO airframes. It remains unclear as to how many F-5Fs were produced for service.

The F-5G

As converted P-38L-5-LOs, the F-5G-6-LO aircraft had a wider variety of photographic reconnaissance wares. Sixty-three F-5Gs were produced at Dallas, Texas.

The FO-1

Assigned Bureau Numbers 01209 through 01212 for its North Africa activities, the U.S. Navy

A 425 mph camera platform, the F-5G was the last version of about 1,000 Photo Lightnings built from the standard P-38 Lightning configuration. The special nose section housed five powerful aerial cameras that took photographs both vertically (downward) and obliquely (sideward). Clear pictures were made at altitudes that ranged from tree-top heights to more than 30,000 feet. The F-5Gs were convertible: USAAF mechanics in the field could interchange their factory-installed camera noses with regular production gun-laden noses. *Lockheed Martin*

procured four F-5B Photo Lightnings for its use and designated them FO-1s. Few of the details regarding them have ever been told.

With Lockheed at Burbank and Consolidated at Nashville, 10,038 P-38/F-4/F-4 Lightning and Photo Lightning aircraft were produced. This was one of the most successful production runs during World War II, and without question, one of the most important ones as well. Ultimately these aircraft were employed for every imaginable duty: from fighter to interceptor to trainer; from bomber to bomber escort to photographic reconnaissance; and even from night fighter to transporter aircraft. Whether better than their contemporaries or not they were a most valuable asset to the allied forces. What began as a scary and dangerous prototype had evolved into a friendly and safe combat aircraft.

This is not the view of a P-38E that an enemy pilot wanted to see. Equipped with a pair of auxiliary drop-type fuel tanks, this Lightning appears to be bearing down on an enemy's six o' clock position for a kill. *Lockheed Martin*

The P-38M Night Lightning saw service during the last weeks of the Pacific war just before VJ Day. As a two-seat, radar-equipped modification of production P-38L-5-LOs, it was 50 mph faster than earlier USAAF night fighters such as the Northrop P-61 Black Widow. Its double mission was to seek and destroy Japanese night bombers and serve as a nocturnal prowler—an aerial battleship packing rockets and bombs. *Lockheed Martin*

Extremely versatile, this version of the P-38 was called the Lightning Droop Snoot and performed as a bombardier. As it happened, Allied fighters flew deep into enemy territory without opposition in late 1944, when the fast-dwindling German fighter force was being conserved to intercept heavy bombardment aircraft only. American ingenuity took advantage of the situation by developing the Droop Snoot leader plane. It was a modified P-38L with an elongated nose carrying a bombardier, who aimed for large formations of Lightnings, each packing 4,000 pounds of bombs. The formations caused extensive damage to enemy installations for numerous months before Luftwaffe fighter pilots learned of the deception. Lockheed engineers developed these unique Droop Snoots at English air bases, and they were later replaced by Lightning Pathfinders that were P-38s equipped with various types of radar systems for even more accurate bombing missions. *Lockheed Martin*

In addition to several test aircraft to develop the P-38M, Lockheed's Modification Center at Dallas, Texas, converted 75 P-38L-5-LOs into Night Lightnings. Their radar system was comprised of the AN/APS-6 unit and was housed in a pod undernose and on centerline as shown on this P-38M in flight. *Lockheed Martin*

Under camouflage, Lockheed's Burbank, California, plant employees are at the Army and Navy E for Excellence award ceremony whereby they were honored for their out-standing contribution to the war effort by building many new and high-quality aircraft for use in World War II. One such aircraft was the P-38/F-4/F-5 series like the one shown near the end of the building, closest to the camera. *Dennis Wrynn Collection*

This is a fine study of a P-38H-5-LO (S/N 42-67079) on a manufacturer's test hop with Tony LeVier at the controls. During the 1942 through 1945 time period, LeVier accumulated more than 1,000 hours flying Lightnings. *Lockheed Martin*

This is the very same factory from above, showing Lockheed's clever concealment effort to create the effect of its factory being part of the natural environment. *Dennis Wrynn Collection*

COLOR GALLERY

This outstanding view of a YP-38 from down under illustrates its overall beauty and grace. When first seen by those without much enthusiasm about airplanes, their appearance must have been a shock. *NASM via Jeff Ethell*

The number two YP-38 (S/N 39-690) service test aircraft as it appeared in the fall of 1940 at Wright Field, Dayton, Ohio. At the time this aircraft was arguably the sleekest looking fighter-type airplane in the world. *USAF/Rene J. Francillon Collection*

In the markings of the 14th FG, 37th FS, this beautifully restored P-38L-5-LO flies near Los Angeles in September 1977 during the Split-S Society's Symposium on the Lightning, 40-plus years after it first flew. *Lockheed Martin*

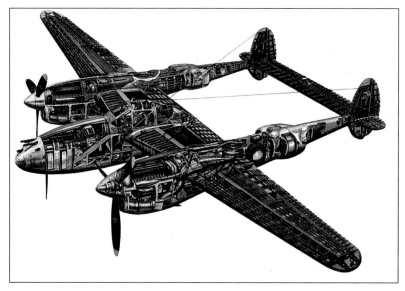

This cutaway, among many other things, illustrates the location of the V-1710 engines employed by the P-38.
Lockheed Martin

A P-38E-LO (S/N 41-1986) is shown on a test flight prior to its modification with lengthened tail booms and raised and reshaped vertical tails to test a proposed twin-float version for operations on water. As proposed water-based fighters, these were never ordered into production. *NASM via Jeff Ethell*

A Lockheed employee tightens one of the P-38's many panels. Slightly ajar is the ammunition storage panel, just above where she is working. This large compartment held the ammunition for the P-38's massive amount of firepower. *Dennis Wyrnn Collection*

As it climbs higher to reach its three other P-38E friends (upper right), this P-38E (S/N 41-2252) was first armed with one 37mm cannon (15 rounds), later replaced with one 20mm cannon (150 rounds). The P-38E has the distinction of being the first major production model (210 built), but, they did not enter the war until they had been brought up to combat standard. *NASM via Jeff Ethell*

Led by a factory-fresh F-5B (S/N 42-67332), a newly built P-38J closely follows. Painted blue to blend-in with the skies, unarmed Photo Lightnings were indeed the fastest photographic reconnaissance aircraft of World War II. Unescorted for the most part, F-4 and F-5 aircraft needed every hit of speed they could get. Armed only with cameras, and flown by more-than- brave pilots, photo Lightnings played a very important role in the war by letting frontline commanders know what they were facing. *Lockheed Martin via Jeff Ethell Collection*

A pair of F-5s belonging to the 7th Photographic Reconnaissance Group are about to take-off from their base in late-1944. *Robert Astrella via Jeff Ethell*

A 7th PRG F-5 (42-68273) as it appeared in 1944. Its blue camouflage paint scheme effectively hid the airplane in-flight as it blended into either blue or grey skies. *Jeff Ethell Collection*

Another Mt. Farm-based F-5, *Tough Kid*, of the 7th PRG as it appeared in 1945. Note sighting bore scope in front of left-hand side windshield. These were used late to better the pilot a better view of what he was to photograph during low-level missions. *Robert Astrella via Jeff Ethell*

* *Peg O' My Heart*, a 318th FG (21st FG earlier) P-38J at Siapan in late-1944. *Campbell Archives via Jeff Ethell*

Posing at their base in China, three P-38s of the 51st FG show off the colors and markings of USAAF aircraft during early 1945. The Lightning in the foreground is a P-38J-10-LO. *USAF/Rene J. Francillon Collection*

This P-38H-1-LO (S/N 42-66644) served with an unknown training unit somewhere in the western United States, circa 1943. Note the Martin B-26 Marauders in the background. *USAF/Rene J. Francillon Collection*

Likewise, this P-38G-10-LO (S/N 42-13579) was located at the very same unknown training base in 1943. Unlike early Lightnings, late model P-38s featured "hub caps" as shown. *USAF/Rene J. Francillon Collection*

This P-38L-5-LO (S/N 44-53232) was restored to appear like former U.S. Air Force Museum staff member Royal D. Frey's 20th FG, 55th FS Lightning he called *Stardust*. With civil registration number N9957F, it is now on display at McGuire AFB, Wrightstown, New Jersey, to honor America's next all-time highest scoring ace Maj. Tom McGuire. It is now shown in the markings of his last P-38—*Puggy V. Lockheed Martin*

Though fuzzy, this is a rare color photo of a P-38-LO of the then 1st PG, 96th PS, on a training flight out of Wright Field in late 1941. The 1st PG (later FG) was the first to receive P-38s. *USAF/Rene J. Francillon Collection*

This P-38H-5-LO belonged to the 8th FG, 80th FS, and was based in New Guinea in 1943. Its crew members included R. E. Devereaux, F. J. Bean, and J. Gunter. The pilot, then Lt. Jay T. Robbins, had seven victories at the time. *USAF/Rene J. Francillon Collection*

Lieutenant Jay T. Robbins acquired 22 kills by war's end; thus, he became an ace four times over. *USAF/Rene J. Francillon Collection*

Here once again you can see the benefit of camouflage to hide Lockheed P-38s from unwanted eyes in the skies above. Here Lockheed test pilot Jimmy Mattern prepares to make still another test hop in a factory-fresh Lightning. *Lockheed Martin via Dave Ostrowski*

CHAPTER FIVE

CHARGED PARTICLES: TEST PILOT TALES

To make the P-38 a viable fighter airplane, numerous Lockheed and USAAF test pilots had to first discover its attributes and idiosyncrasies. This was done throughout the war, and in fact, by late 1942, these test pilots had already made more than 5,500 flights in P-38s with only one accident. Sharing their acquired knowledge, these are some of their stories:

Report on P-38s in the ETO (European Theater of Operation)

by Lockheed Engineering Test Pilot Tony LeVier:

"Having just returned from a four-month mission to England on 29 May 1944 where I had been testing and demonstrating some of the new improvements on our P-38Js, I filed the following report:"

This picture of Civilian Air Patrol Cpl. James W. Pace illustrates the eagerness of those many young men wanting to fly combat missions against the Axis. He is about to make his first advanced training flight. Before USAAF pilots ever got the chance to fly P-38s in combat, they too had to make numerous advanced training flights in AT-6s. *U.S. Air Force via Rockwell*

Immediately upon arriving in England I proceeded to 55th FG Headquarters at Nuthamstead, an air base in East Anglia, north of London, where conditions were pretty grim as far as their P-38s were concerned. They had just received their first P-38Js and had no operational information on them. Their lack of information concerning correct power combinations was appalling.

For combat missions some pilots were using anywhere from 2,000rpm to 3,000rpm with whatever manifold pressure that would give them their desired air speed. Some of these pilots were blowing up their engines with high manifold pressure and critically low rpm, while others were running out of gas and failing to complete missions because of such power combinations for continual

Highly regarded as a pilot's pilot, Tony LeVier was one of the many Lockheed test pilots who helped make the Lightnings safer planes for USAAF combat pilots. Shown with his privately-owned P-38L—the first Lightning to be procured (23 January 1946) from the Kingman, Arizona, depot after the war for $1,200—LeVier with an average speed of 370.193 mph, finished second in the 1946 Thompson Trophy Race. In the 1947 Sohio Race, with an average speed of 360.866 mph, his red number three Lightning placed first. Then, after finishing fifth in the 1947 Thompson Trophy Race, he sold it to the late Byron Roche. Note early P/F-8OA in the background. *Lockheed Martin via Tony LeVier*

The famed ventriloquist Edgar Bergen with his smart-alecky Charlie McCarthy dummy visited Wright AAF in early 1942. While there, he was of course given VIP treatment while learning some things about the Lightning. With them—in front of the ninth YP-38 (S/N 39-697)—are two flight-test pilots and their commanding officer. P-38 flight-test activities were carried out mostly by Lockheed, Muroc AAF, Eglin AAF, and Wright AAF personnel in California, Florida, and Ohio. *Dave Ostrowski Collection*

cruise at 2,800 rpm with 24 inches manifold pressure. Many returned with hardly more than a cupful of gas remaining in their tanks, while others were forced to bail out over enemy territory.

The reason they were cruising at 2,600, 2,800, and even 3,000 rpm was that somewhere along the line they had been taught to use high rpm and low manifold pressure. They were under the impression that should they get jumped by a Jerry they could get their power faster if they already had their engines running at high rpm.

The fact is you can get your power quicker if you have a low rpm and a high boost which gives you a higher turbosupercharger speed. With the turbosuperchargers already putting out high boost you only have to increase your engine rpm to get your desired power.

Rather than add to their confusion with power curves and range charts we devised the following rule of thumb for their long range mis-

sions. It is simple and easy to remember and insures maximum engine efficiency/fuel economy: USE 2,300RPM AND 36IN MANIFOLD PRESSURE AS THE MAXIMUM FOR AUTO LEAN AND CRUISE CONDITIONS. IN REDUCING POWER FROM THIS SETTING, REDUCE 1/2IN TO 1IN FOR EACH 100RPM; FOR GOING ABOVE THIS SETTING PUT YOUR MIXTURE IN AUTO RICH AND INCREASE THE MANIFOLD PRESSURE 2IN FOR EACH 100RPM.

After using this rule the boys marveled at their increased range. Some were returning from four-hour missions with as much as 150 to 200 gallons of fuel left. Quite a bit more than the cupfuls they had been returning with!

The Boys Have What It Takes
Don't think for a New York second that the

Lockheed test pilot Jimmy Mattern illustrates the high-altitude oxygen mask similar to the one worn by Lockheed test pilot Joe Towle on 30 April 1943 when he unofficially broke the U.S. altitude record while flying a P-38 to 44,940 feet. As reported on 20 July 1943, Towle, with USAAF Col. Randolph Lovelace (chief of the USAAF's aeromedical laboratory at Wright AAF) in the P-38's piggyback seat, were trying out a new mask that forced oxygen into the lungs to permit much higher flights than with then conventional oxygen masks. Towle recalled, "We took off from Burbank . . . in an attempt to test the mask at 45,000 feet. Just sixty feet short of our goal, trouble developed in the outside temperature gauge. We landed a little more than an hour after our takeoff. The masks, which worked perfectly during this test, are now being used by the USAAF on all of its high altitude aircraft, including the [Boeing] B-29s." The 44,940 foot altitude was at the time the highest mark ever achieved by a reciprocating engine airplane in the United States. *Dave Ostrowski Collection*

Forty years after the XP-38's first flight, three major players in the Lightning's success story were honored at the 1977 Historical Symposium. Pictured in front of David Tallichet's P-38L are left-to-right: Brig. Gen. Benjamin S. Kelsey, USAF (Ret.), who made the first flight on the XP-38; Clarence L. Johnson who, along with Hall L. Hibbard and others, designed the Lightning; and Anthony W. LeVier, who was one of the major contributors to its successful engineering changes and flight-test operations. *Lockheed Martin*

boys flying '38s over there are a bunch of green-horns who know nothing about flying. Enough can't be said about their flying abilities and raw courage. I'm merely mentioning certain cases that were encountered in which they were not too clear on some procedures.

I could go on forever reporting stories that were told to me of unbelievable experiences. Take the case of one '38 pilot that was flying at low altitude and caught a 20mm cannon slug in his nose armament section. It blew the armament bay access panels open and folded them back over the windshield.

He called to his flight leader and told him something had happened and he was unable to see forward from the cockpit. The flight leader instructed him to get some altitude and continue on instruments. With the rest of his squadron forming an escort he flew over 100 miles back and, with a careful talkdown by his flight leader, made a safe landing at his base.

It is quite common to see boys coming back with two or three feet of wing blown off. And I talked with guys coming back from flights where the temperature at altitude was as low as 60 to 70 degrees below zero—so cold that their elevator trim tabs and even the gasoline selector valves froze up. There were cases where pilots were forced to make emergency landings because they

Lockheed chief engineering test pilot Milo Burcham discusses the performance of the then new maneuvering flaps with Kelly Johnson after his first flaps-evaluation flight out of Burbank. *Lockheed Martin*

Standing atop the left wing of YIPPEE—a P-38J and the 5,000th Lightning built—Mile Burcham prepares to make its first flight in the spring of 1944. At 5,000 built, this milestone airplane would be followed by still another 5,038 P-38s. *Lockheed Martin*

were unable to switch to a full fuel tank due to their hands becoming too cold and the selector valves freezing solid.

The selector valve problem was improved by attaching a Tee handle on each selector that now allows a good grip, and some recommendations to the factory were made to improve the '38's heating system.

Turbosupercharger Trouble

The day after I arrived at another base in England some P-38 pilots who had been escorting Forts [Boeing B-17 Flying Fortress bombers] over mainland Europe reported a "sort of engine trouble."

When pinned down they said their engines had been surging and momentarily cutting out while they were flying at altitude under reduced power. They passed it off saying, "It's probably caused by some extra low octane gas."

But after further discussion with the boys I suddenly remembered a series of tests we had run back home during flight-test operations for proper turbosupercharger settings. As I recalled, the symptoms were very similar.

So I obtained permission from the 55th FG commanding officer to test a P-38 at altitude for proper turbosupercharger operation, and sure enough, the turbosupercharger regulator on the left engine was so rigged that the resulting back pressure and high turbosupercharger wheel speed

caused the airflow to the engine to surge, resulting in erratic operation and inability to pull power.

Upon landing, I reported the trouble and recommended that each Lightning driver be given the following procedure for checking his '38 at altitude for proper turbosupercharger operation: At 30,000 feet set your rpm at 2,600 and 37 inches manifold pressure and back off slowly on the power down to 10 to 15 inches manifold pressure. While doing this fix your eyes on the manifold pressure and note if there is the slightest engine failure or surging. Record the exact manifold pressure at which this surging occurs.

Now repeat the process beginning with 2,300rpm and 37 inches manifold pressure, and again record the boost at which the surging occurs. (At this lower rpm it should occur 2 or 3 inches higher.)

If, after you've completed this procedure, either of the recorded manifold pressures are above 22 inches, it indicates that the turbosupercharger regulator is set improperly. Tell your mechanic the boost at which the roughness occurred and he will make the necessary adjustments.

All in All

All in all we can be proud of our P-38 fighters and their contribution towards complete victory—but don't forget the fellas over there that are flying them.

In this fine study of the number one YP-38 (S/N 39-689), Lockheed test pilot Marshall Headle poses for a photo-shoot prior to first flight on 18 September 1940. Unlike subsequent production Lightnings, the YP-38 as shown featured a one-piece windscreen. Other new features included redesigned engine nacelles to house the oil cooler air scoops beneath the props and larger Prestone coolant radiators/air scoops aft of the improved F series Allison V-1710 engines. *Lockheed Martin*

It isn't a picnic that they are over there, not by any stretch of the imagination, and from a flying standpoint they are really on the ball. From my discussion here you might get the idea that I went over there and taught them to fly. It was quite the contrary. I learned plenty about flying during my brief stay in the ETO and my hat is off to all the boys flying in combat—whether a '38 driver or not. It requires intelligence, patriotism, and plenty of good old-fashioned guts.

Spin Characteristics of the P-38
by Lockheed Engineering Test Pilot Herman R. "Fish" Salmon

While visiting training bases we are frequently asked about the spin characteristics of

the P-38. Such questions as "Have you ever spun a '38?" and "How do you get a '38 out of a spin?" indicate that there is a little confusion about the spin characteristics of the Lightning.

Positive Spin Recovery Procedure
To begin, during flight-test operations, I spun a P-38L 28 times over Muroc Army Air Field [now Edwards Air Force Base] under every possible condition, including a range of CG [center of gravity] from 27 percent forward to 32 percent aftward—landing gear up and down, with dive flaps extended and not extended, on one engine, and with power on and off.

It doesn't matter what configuration the Lightning is in when the spin is started, it always develops a steady nose-down spin after the fourth turn (if you allow it to go that far) from which recovery is a cinch.

Because of the '38's excellent stall characteristics it is unlikely that you will find yourself in an inadvertent spin, but should the unexpected happen, or should you try spinning as an evasive maneuver, here are some solutions we discovered for easy, rapid recovery:

1. Don't get excited—even if you are thrown about in the cockpit or find it difficult to orient yourself with the ground.

2. Cut back the power on both engines, and simultaneously kick full rudder[s] against the spin.

3. Clean up the airplane by raising dive flaps, maneuvering flaps and landing gear if extended. (The airplane will recover with flaps down but we found it takes about one turn longer.)

4. Wait far at least one-half turn with the rudder[s] full against the spin and the elevator back, before moving the control column forward.

5. As the rate of rotation decreases, move the control column forward toward the neutral position. If you have difficulty in moving the control column forward it indicates that your rate of rotation is too fast. Don't fight the column forward—just wait a little longer, still holding the rudder pedals against the stops.

6. As the central column approaches neutral, the spin will stop and you will find yourself in a steep nose-down pitch attitude at a low airspeed.

7. When the speed increases to about 150 mph, perform a gradual pullout. If you pull out too sharply, you might stall and spin off in the opposite direction.

Thus the procedure for spin recovery in a '38 is basically the same as that learned back in primary flying training. But there is one essential difference—YOU MUST WAIT FOR AT LEAST A HALF A TURN AFTER KICKING RUDDER[S] AGAINST THE SPIN BEFORE MOVING THE CONTROL COLUMN FORWARD. This rule of thumb is absolutely imperative!

Dive Flaps

by Lockheed Production Test Pilot Nick Nicholson

Incredible as it may sound, until the installation of dive flaps the P-38s performance was limited because it flew too fast. That is, it accelerated so rapidly in a dive that a pilot might easily get into the compressibility speed range in a matter of seconds.

German Air Force [Luftwaffe] FW-190 and Me-109 fighter pilots recognized this limitation of the '38 to their advantage, and disengaged at will by merely diving steeply away from it. At 30,000 feet a '38 pilot without dive flaps, desiring to get

P-38 flight-test evaluations were not only numerous but varied. Here, shown at Wright AAF, is the first production P-38-LO (S/N 40-744), later redesignated RP-38 (R for restricted: not to be used in combat). With a second cockpit on its left boom, this Lightning was used by the aeromedical laboratory in a project to study the effect of maneuvers on a person sitting a good distance from the center of gravity in anticipation of the forthcoming North American XP-82 Twin Mustang. Tested in part by then 1st Lt. Glen W. Edwards, the off-set was found to have no particular ill effects. Later, Capt. Edwards—killed on 5 June 1948 in the crash of a Northrop YB-49 Flying Wing bomber—was immortalized when Muroc was renamed Edwards Air Force Base. *AFFTC/HO via Ray Puffer*

In the first scene, approaching a gunnery target on a range at Muroc AAF over a Boeing B-17, Douglas B-23, and P-38s, a Lightning prepares to fire its nose-mounted array of four .50 calibre machine guns and one 20mm cannon: in scene two, it has successfully hit the target and flies on. Muroc, first established as a bombardment and gunnery practices base, is now Edwards AFB, home of the USAF's Flight Test Center. *AFFTC/HO via Ray Puffer*

down to 10,000 feet in a hurry was limited to a maximum 15 degree dive angle at rated power if he wanted to avoid compressibility.

P-38 pilots were instructed to observe placard dive speeds and angles, and to watch for nose heaviness and buffeting which are the first indications of compressibility.

But all of this is changed now. With the new dive flaps extended you can push-over or peel-off from 30,000 feet and pull out without difficulty at any altitude. Whereas 15 degrees was the maximum angle for extended dives without the dive flaps, you can now safely dive with power OFF at 45 degrees without fear of compressibility.

Incidentally, when we talk about 45 degrees we mean an accurately measured angle of 45 degrees. To the pilot looking over the nose, it will seem as if the dive angle is closer to 80 degrees. This has been the universal reaction of all '38 pilots when checking their judgment against our dive indicator instrumentation.

We remember when the first tests on the dive flaps were being run. One pilot caused quite a stir in the pilot house when he came down and stated that he had just Split-S'ed from 30,000 feet down to 6,000 feet, and pulled out without any difficulty. That sounded almost like another one of those 800 mph stories to some of us. But his story was true. After the dive flaps were installed on all production P-38s, we had our chance to learn for ourselves.

Takeoffs

by Lockheed Test Pilot Jimmy Mattern and Lockheed Engineering Test Pilot Mile Burcham

First of all before takeoff we lock the top hatch and make darn sure that both sliding windows are securely closed, for if they are left open even a little an annoying buffeting will be experienced.

To make sure that the mechanic gassed her up, we check all tanks and when carrying a full load, always take off on the front tanks. It may be that gas rationing has made us supersensitive on this subject, but it pays dividends.

After the usual engine warm-up and magneto check, we see that the propeller selector switch is in the automatic position and try the governors [rev up the engines] to make sure they are really governing.

Now, on the P-38s equipped with external tanks, Mile Burcham says: Before takeoff I always place the drop tanks' switch in the safe position and the drop tank selectors on, so that if necessary I can lose the tanks by hitting the drop tank release button. This comes in pretty handy in case of single engine failure on takeoff.

On normal takeoffs we use no flaps but we do use, always, maximum allowable manifold pres-

sure. To do this, brakes are held with the balls of the feet, rather than with the toes, and both throttles are advanced to get the boost up. This precaution at the head of the runway is important, for it gets those turbos running for takeoff power and it also allows the props to reach the governing limit of 3,000 rpm at the start of the run. Thus, we know if the props are going to "run wild" while there is still time to abort takeoff.

With the maximum manifold pressure and without flaps the P-38 takes off at between 90 and 110 mph indicated, but due to the tricycle gear, the ship has no tendency to fly itself; so, at 70 mph indicated we ease the column back and at 90 to 110 mph pull back hard to break ground. The gear is upped immediately and the ship is committed to flight, by which time we will be well above the single engine flying speed of 120 mph indicated. Normal takeoffs are made without flaps in order to reach this single engine operation quickly. We use 50 percent flaps or more for short fields, muddy, or sandy ground, or when obstacles are encountered. After takeoff the normal power rating is 37 inches manifold pressure and 2,600 rpm.

Single Engine Procedure

by Lockheed Engineering Test Pilot Joe Towle

Whenever combat pilots "work over" P-38s, sooner or later single-engine flight procedure is brought up; and we '38 test pilots are no exception. The other day when the chief of flight-test operations heard us "flying" around the waiting room on single engine, he broke up our little session by saying: "There's a right and wrong way of doing everything—particularly flying on one engine. Our engineers have spent many, many hours checking the best procedures for single engine operation, and it's about time you fellows get acquainted with their findings. It isn't hard to fly on one engine—it's just knowing how to do it. After all, didn't most or all of you learn how to fly on single engine aircraft?!"

When an engine quits, reduce the power on the live engine and correct yaw [nose-left, nose-right and vice versa] with hard opposite rudder[s]; then increase power as much as you can hold. The dead engine's mixture control should be set to idle cut-off, to reduce fire hazard by stopping the flow of fuel. Set the feathering switch to full-feather, and

NEXT PAGES
Lockheed test pilot Jim White is about to wring out yet another production Lightning, in this case one of 790 P-38J-105 (S/N 42-68008). The J-model, powered by 1,600 horsepower (war emergency power rating) V-1710-89/-91s, had an impressive top speed of 410 mph at 25,000 feet. *Dave Ostrowski Collection*

2519

P-38 gunnery evaluations were also conducted at Eglin AAF (now Eglin AFB) in Florida. Here a late-model P-38 flies low in a simulated gire-firing pass at what appears to be a near-new target. *Mark Adamic Collection*

pull the throttle back to close. That's all there is to getting set for single engine flight.

If the flight is going to be for any duration though, you'll find that the following operations make for safer and better flying: turn off the booster pump for the dead engine, trim the rudder tab, close the tank selector valve, the Prestone shutter, and the oil cooler flap of the dead engine.

Don't burn up your good engine—31 inches of mercury with 2,300 rpm is satisfactory cruising power, and for single engine climb, 37 inches with 2,600 rpm is recommended. The use of more power is unnecessary. Single engine power stall occurs at 90 mph indicated, and you will experience a big change in directional trim along with change in speed, comparable to the torque effect in single engine aircraft.

Single engine landings are a cinch—but never count on a twin engine plane maintaining altitude with both the landing gear and flaps full-down. Once full flaps are extended the landing must be made, so never extend the flaps 100 percent unless you know the landing is "in the bag."

Lastly, and importantly, don't be afraid to lose an engine—remember you still have a mighty fine single engine plane in your hands.

Dive Characteristics
by Lockheed Test Pilot Lewis Parker

Reports received from Lockheed technical-field representatives indicate that there are many up and coming combat pilots who privately consider themselves as Hot Pilots. They tell you how easy it is to put a '38's nose straight down and buzz their gal's house so fast that the prop wash will blow off the roof shingles. These HPs do so much hanger flying that some begin to believe their own stories, and before long their reputations make headlines before they do—in the form of crash reports. We were visiting an advanced flight training school recently and one of these HPs was burning up the ready room

On what appears to be a hot day at Burbank, maintenance workers prepare an F-5 Photo Lightning for a Lockheed production flight-test pilot's arrival. Soon, after a single flight, the airplane (if satisfactory) will be delivered to the USAAF. *Lockheed Martin*

with tales of his ability to pull out of a dive lower than any other guy in the class.

We asked if he could tell us how much altitude he'd need to bring his '38 out of a 300 mph dive, if it required 800 feet to pull out of a similar dive at 200 mph. His answer of 1,200 feet would have put him about 600 feet underground. You see, he had forgotten the basic rule: For a given G-load a plane going twice as fast needs four times the room to recover from a dive. As the ratio of dive speeds increases from two-, three-, or four-to-one, the ratio of the corresponding distance required to regain level-attitude flight is four-, nine-, and sixteen-to-one at a given acceleration.

To insure against pilot error in judging distance we have a rule which sets 10,000 feet as the minimum altitude for dive tests, loops, and so on. This does not mean that it is dangerous to go under this altitude, but it does give you a healthy padding, in case an emergency should

arise. Due to the P-38s rapid acceleration in a dive, the ground comes up awfully fast. That's why a dive limit placard is in the cockpit—check it—obey it. For without doing so, the ground will smack you in your face.

P-38 Combat Experience

After returning to the United States, one Air Force Captain that served in North Africa and Sicily had this to tell Lockheed about his P-38 combat experience:

"The chief fighting characteristic of the P-38, aside from its terrific firepower, is its high-altitude capability. And because of its excellent performance at high altitude, the strategy for combat, he said, is to force the aerial battle upward whenever possible. For as the altitude increases the '38 gains the advantage over the Jerry planes not designed for the thinner air.

"Another point of interest is that the P-38 could not only climb higher, but faster than any of the

Captain John S. Litchfield, pilot, and his crew chief T/Sgt. Robert Elkins pose beside their P-38, *Sweet Pea*, in Italy, circa 1944. *USAF 1FW/HO*

One P-38 of the 1st FG, loaded with bombs, is ready to leave on yet another mission from its base in Italy. *USAF 1FW/HO*

German fighters I encountered. This is important, and as a result of this characteristic an effective combat technique has been developed—that of outclimbing the enemy, and when he stalls out, just rolling over and picking him off.

"Because of the P-38's counter-rotating propellers there is no torque and no tendency to slip off on either wing at the top of your climb. As a result you can obtain every bit of the maximum climb. Because of torque, most single engine fighters tend to slip off just below their maximum ceiling, thus leaving themselves wide open for a P-38 pilot who waits for this moment overhead, and then peels off for the kill.

"Another maneuver I used is the use of the twin rudders to increase rate of roll. Just give them a good kick while rolling and you'll find your rate of roll speeded up considerably, which is a good thing in combat."

Maneuvers
by Lockheed Test Pilot Ray Meskimen

Production hops, acceptance flights, and occasional delivery flights are pretty dull compared to the combat action our USAAF fellows get. We [Lockheed flight-test personnel] know there's little comparison, but daily flights in each new '38 off the assembly line enable us to become thoroughly familiar with the limitations of the Lightning aircraft.

The P-38's maneuverability is a much discussed subject in ready-rooms on every fighting front. The best way to get the answer for yourself is to take a '38 up and practice, practice, practice. As you become more familiar with the plane, you'll be more amazed with its ability to climb, bank, and pull out, even with one engine feathered. Only through practice and repetition of Immelmans, slow rolls, and stalls can you truly learn what is meant by the Lightning's maneuverability. Usually, the individual's physical and mental limitations—not the plane's limitations—are factors that govern combat maneuverability. In many cases the plane will take a lot more than you can stand. Therefore, recognize your own limitations, know how many Gs you can stand, and for how long. Be so familiar with your plane that you automatically react to a situation despite the gray haze that creeps before your eyes in a sharp pull out.

I'd like to pass on some hints that may be of value to you. You see, we slip out over the Mojave Desert occasionally and have our own little rat races, and once in a while two of us will get together and sweat out a simulated dogfight. By the way, these are not exactly a novelty for some of us who played around with live bullets over France in the last World War.

With a pair of drop tanks, this P-38E of the 1st FG departs its base in Italy for an escort mission with B-24s. *USAF 1FW/HO*

High-speed fighters today have a high wing loading and we know that this increases the turning radius. This condition has been improved on the '38 by the use of maneuvering flaps—also called dive or combat flaps. There is a maneuvering flap stop on the flap controls which extends the flaps 50 percent. These should not be extended at speeds in excess of 250 mph, for there is danger of structural failure if this limitation is disregarded.

Maneuvering flaps increase your lift, thus assisting you in making tighter turns. For greatest maneuverability we have found that the maneuvering flaps should be extended only long enough to complete the particular maneuver and then be retracted immediately. For example, in an effort to stay on an enemy's six o'clock [tail], you might feel—in a tight turn—the buffeting which is characteristic of an accelerated stall. You can "reef" her in and tighten your turn by extending the maneuvering flaps until you've completed the maneuver, then retract them. By doing so immediately, little air speed is lost, and the plane is set again for maximum operations.

Don't get caught with your flaps down for any length of time in combat; the reason being that with them down you can unknowingly get down to such low speeds that all the power in the world won't do you much good should you get jumped and need sudden acceleration. From 25,000 to 35,000 feet the maneuvering flaps become increasingly helpful. Due to the thinness of the air you can't turn as sharp, nor can you pull as many Gs as can be done below 20,000 feet. As you go higher you find that you are stalling more frequently, but you'll be surprised at the increased maneuverability resulting from the extension of your flaps at the higher altitudes.

In combat, use the Lightning's superior speed and climb abilities to keep you on top of the enemy.

You all know that the '38's rate of climb is about the same from 140 to 180 mph. This range relieves you of keeping your eyes glued to the air speed indicator when you're trying to get up there the fastest; and the maximum of 180 mph gives you the dual advantage of not only getting upstairs faster, but also covering more distance in the same time than your enemy, whose best climbing speeds may be 145 to 150 mph.

On the P-38J model, where the intercoolers are in the engine nacelles, open them fully for long, high-power climbs in order that the carburetor air temperatures are kept down, thus

A large formation of 1st FG P-38s buzz the field as they return to their base after escorting B-24s from Austria. *USAF 1FW/HO*

giving more power and avoiding detonation. For level-attitude flights and ordinary maneuvers, keep them closed because they will knock at least 15 mph off your top speed. At climbing speeds, the increased power obtained by keeping the carburetor air temperatures down more than offsets the increased drag.

Caution must be used above 25,000 feet not to overspeed your turbosuperchargers. Know your maximum boost for given altitudes and do not exceed these figures. On late models of the '38 there are Turbo Overspeed Warning Lights which flicker when the maximum is approached and which stay on when the maximum is reached.

In closing, the importance of maneuvers cannot be over-emphasized. The more you know about them the better your chances are in combat. As a fighting unit, the pilot and his '38 are only as strong as their greatest limitation, be it mechanical or human.

Center of Gravity (CG)

by USAAF Test Pilot Lt. Col. Clarence A. Shoop

In the old days when we flew by the seat of our pants and the grace of God we scoffed at new-fangled instruments, weight and balance charts, and the like. If the plane looked OK and we figured there was an even chance of making it, we took her off (or went through a barbed-wire fence, which was a trademark of the cow pastures we used for air strips).

What a different gang we are today. Only this morning one of the boys who barnstormed in a Curtiss JN-4 Jenny squawked a plane because she had too great a rearward CG. Ridiculous, you say? No, it isn't. The '38 is a fighter pilot's fighter and if you expect the best performance you first must ensure that the plane is in perfect fighting trim. All the power, ammunition, and the armor plate won't be much help in combat if your plane is unstable and you find yourself fighting both the plane and the enemy.

However, due to the careful designing of our engineers, you fellows in combat do not have to worry too much about CG because the '38 with a full complement of guns, ammunition and fuel (including external reserve tanks) has a CG within the permissible range. Unless some forgetful mechanic leaves his tool box in the baggage com-

91

partment or you take off without one of your guns (which is unlikely), the plane's CG will not exceed its limitations.

We have become very CG conscious around here because we frequently flight-test new Lightnings minus guns/cannon and ammunition; and, if the crew chief has his mind on the little blond haired timekeeper rather than securely stowing compensating ballast in the nose, we are liable to stall out before getting our landing gear and flaps up. We make a practice of checking the weight and balance chart and also inspecting the baggage compartment in the right boom before each flight. We figure it pays to do so.

Teamwork

by USAAF Lt. William L. Bolton

In April 1943, a squadron of P-38s were on the way out to a German target. I, the flight's element leader, developed electrical trouble and was forced to turn back for home base. My wingman, Lt. Edwin H. Schneider, stayed with me.

On our way home over enemy territory over North Africa, we got jumped by seven German fighters—four Me-109s and three FW-190s. During the dogfight that ensued, I got on the tail of and destroyed one of the '109s.

At the same time a '190 pulled in behind and below my '38. The remaining five fighters were on Schneider's tail. But, seeing the '190 on my tail— with complete disregard of his own safety—he went after and destroyed the plane on my tail. After a running dogfight we succeeded in evading the other five German fighters and returned safely to our home base.

Thus, we especially know the value of teamwork. And for my wingman's valiant action to save my butt, he received the Distinguished Flying Cross.

Decoys Are Death

by USAAF Office of Flying Safety

Don't let the "sitter" fool you! Nine times out of ten he's a decoy for the rest of his squadron.

In July 1943, a squadron of P-38s escorted a group of B-17s to a target in Italy. On the way out, one of the fighters reported a lone Me-109 flying at the same altitude at three o'clock, about one-quarter of a mile away. He looked like a "sitter," but the squadron kept on minding its own business of escorting the B-17s.

Soon, another '38 reported the presence of eight other '109s at six o'clock high. One '38 pilot, who apparently didn't hear the radio reports, fell for the come-on tactic of the lone '109 and peeled off to get him. He was lucky enough to hit the German with a good burst and saw him going down, but he didn't see the eight other '109s who had been waiting for one or more of the '38s to get itchy trigger fingers. In less than five seconds, he was trapped, and his plane was destroyed. He bailed-out over enemy territory, and if he wasn't killed on capture, he must be a prisoner of war.

The bottom line: to make sure you hear all reports during a mission, check your radio while you are still on the ground; stay in formation; don't go off on your own: the one-man army idea may get you glory, but you may not be there to hear about it.

In summation, not being there, one can only imagine how exciting and/or boring it must have been for the numerous Lockheed and USAAF pilots to flight-test thousands of P-38, F-4, and F-5 aircraft between 1940 and 1945. But without their countless contributions and hardships during that time period, whereby they made a highly advanced (if not radical) fighter plane safe, the documented success of these aircraft would never have come about. This breed of pilots have more than earned the respect they now enjoy.

Lieutenant Francis in his F-5B-1-LO, *Sniffles* (S/N 42-68301) over Panda, India, on his 40th mission in a late-1943. He later failed to return and was listed as missing in action. *Ken Sumney via Jeff Ethell*

P-38s of either the 449th or 459th FSs are escorting B-25s of the 12th Bombardment Group in 1944 over India. *Mark Adamic Collection*

Numerous F-5s of the 41st PRS at North Field, Guam, in mid-1945. *Mark Adamic Collection*

Inverted Christmas tree–type rocket launchers with ten five-inch-diameter unguided rockets on a late model P-38 which is taxiing for a take off on a development flight out of Burbank. These launchers were installed as standard equipment during the last several months of Lightning production. *Lockheed via Dave Ostrowski*

A fine profile study of a P-38F (S/N 41-7632) at Wright Field sometime in 1942. *USAF via Dave Ostrowski*

Excellent close-up view of an F-5G Photo Lightning (S/N 44-23277), which due to war's end, was never delivered to the USAAF. *Dave Ostrowski collection*

CHAPTER SIX

LIGHTNING FROM HELL: COMBAT OPERATIONS

During aerial combat against the very best fighter-type aircraft in the world, the P-38, with its awesome array of nose-mounted firepower, was a dedicated follower of fashion. Fashion being victory after victory. Sporting four machine guns and a cannon, once an enemy fighter was in its gunsight, there was no escape. In fact, on numerous occasions, enemy fighter pilots abandoned their aircraft before a Lightning opened fire upon them. Still these very same enemy fighter planes, if properly flown by pilots with heart, were formidable air-to-air combatants indeed. Some of these fighters included: the Messerschmitt Bf-109 and Focke Wulf FW-190 of Germany; the Caproni Vizzola F.4 of Italy; the Mitsubishi A6M Zero, Mitsubishi JIM Raiden, Nakajima Ki-27 Otsu, Nakajima Ki-44 Shoki, Kawanishi N1K2 Shiden, and the Kawasaki Ki-61 Hien of Japan.

With a partner nearby, this P-38H-5 (S/N 42-66765) of 78th FG, 82nd FS, is on patrol over North Africa in early 1943 just before the 78th FG transitioned to P-47s. *Dave Ostrowski Collection*

Nevertheless, in every theater of operation, the P-38 for the most part, prevailed over every one of them. For it truly was as the adage goes "a fighter pilot's fighter." And in today's jargon, the "Lightning from hell."

Designed, developed and in production by mid-1941, beginning with a 27th FS, 1st FG, P-38F piloted by USAAF 2nd Lt. Elza P. Shaham, a Lightning teamed-up with a 33rd FS Curtiss P-40C Warhawk to achieve the first USAAF kill over Germany's feared Luftwaffe when they flew out of their base in Iceland and downed a FW 200 Condor over the North Atlantic. And with that first kill on 14 August 1941, the P-38 had finally justified its long-argued existence. Some four years later, with many more kills to its credit, the Lightning had become a star fighter in the first degree. Temporarily dubbed Atlanta by Lock-

With a Republic P-47 Thunderbolt in the background, a P-38B-5 (S/N 42-6790) of the 8th AF's 55th FG poses at an air base at Nuthamstead, England, in November 1943. *Mark Adamic Collection*

This 8th AF P-38E shares an English air base with Douglas A-20 Havocs. Featuring more rounded and less pointed propeller hub spinners (compare with the XP- and YP-38s), the E model had a top speed of 390 mph at 25,000 feet and a rate of climb of 3,076 feet per minute. *Dave Ostrowski Collection*

heed (it was the British name Lightning that stuck), the P-38 is considered by many to be the overall best fighter of World War II.

P-38s in Action

One day after 7 December 1941, when the United States declared war on Japan for its unprovoked attacks on Pearl Harbor, Hawaii, Guam, and the Philippine Islands, Germany and Italy declared war on America. Four days later on 11 December, the United States declared war on those countries and World War II began.

At that time, as far as P-38s and their pilots and crews were concerned, it was not yet time to go off to war. For at that time, due to unavailability of combat-ready Lightnings, it was too soon to avail themselves. Eight months later, with P-38Fs on hand and ready for combat, Lightnings departed their U.S. bases for the ETO. And by August 1942, four squadrons of two

Nellie Ann was a P-38J-15 assigned to the 15th AF, 1st FG, 27th FS. Flying high over Italy circa 1944, this P-38 and many others not only pursued and destroyed enemy planes but straffed and bombed ground- and sea-based targets. *USAF via Jeff Ethell*

groups (the 1st and 14th Fighter Groups; Pursuit Group prior to May 1942) were in the ETO. Two more squadrons of these three-squadron groups would arrive soon after; each group having 111-126 airplanes and 108-126 crews. Thus, as far as the 1st and 14th Fighter Groups were concerned, 222-252 airplanes each with 216-252 crews each.

As you can see, counting spare planes and crews, P-38 FGs and their FSs were heavily armed and manned.

Beginning in June 1941, in an operation called Bolero, the USAAF started deploying combat-ready P-38F-1-LOs to Great Britain. Operated by the 1st and 14th FGs, these Lightnings had to fly from Maine to the United Kingdom by way of Goose Bay, Labrador, to Greenland (code named Blue West One), to Reykjavik, Iceland, to Prestwick, Scotland, and on to their assigned bases. These aircraft, fitted with two 150 gallon drop tanks, were the first single-seat fighters to cross the Atlantic Ocean. Two of these FGs' squadrons, the 27th FS of the 1st FG and the 50th FS of the 14th FG, remained in Iceland to back-up the 33rd FS's P-40Cs.

Following a number of sorties (about 350) without meeting any enemy Luftwaffe aircraft, the 1st and 14th FGs of the 8th AF were ordered to North Africa under 12th AF command. In addition, after its arrival to Northern Ireland in November 1942, the 8th AF's 82nd FG was ordered to join them. By 19 November 1942, these three FG's were in action beginning with the 1st FGs escort mission with B-17s to bomb El Aquina Field at Tunis, Tunisia. The North African campaign ended on 13 May 1943, and these three FGs equipped with P-38s were a most important part of that win against the Axis. And on 1 November 1943 these three P-38 Groups were transferred to the 15th AF. With 37 aces among them, including 1st Lt. W. J. Sloan (82nd FG) with twelve kills, these three FGs alone had proved the value of the Lightning.

After they had established air superiority over Northern Africa and the southern Mediterranean Sea areas, and after they had been assigned to the 12th AF, these 1st FG, 14th FG, and 82nd FG Lightnings were used mostly as B-17 and B-24 bomber escorts on raids on enemy targets in the Balkans, Greece, Italy, France, Austria, southern Germany, and the oil refinery at Ploesti, Rumania. At war's end, having fought in both the North African and MTO campaigns, the three FGs had produced 28 aces.

To bolster the 8th AF in the ETO, the 55th FG arrived at Nuthampstead in Hertfordshire, Eng-

This P-38J-15 (S/N 44-23094) named *Little Mickey* was operated by the 21st FG, 72nd FS at Mokolea, Hawaii. Hawaii-based Lightnings were operated by the 7th AF; two other FSs—the 46th and the 531st—made up the rest of the 21st FG. *Bill Bradbury via Robert F. Dorr*

land, in September 1943. Its squadrons, flying P-38Hs, started operations on 15 October 1943; they converted to P-38Js in December, 1943. Three more P-38 FGs—the 20th FG, 364th FG, and 479th FG—joined the 55th FG by May 1944.

On 3 March 1944, while escorting B-17s to Berlin, Germany, the P-38Js of the 55th FG became the first fighter aircraft to complete that 1,300 mile round trip with their onboard fuel supply. Thus, as a bomber escort fighter, the Lightning had beaten the Republic P-47 Thunderbolt and the North American P-51 Mustang to the punch. The P-38's long range capability had been proved much earlier when, in early 1942, Lockheed test pilot Milo Burcham had flown a P-38F equipped with two 150 gallon drop tanks 3,100 miles without stopping to refuel. Later, two larger 310 gallon drop tanks were carried and range increased substantially. This improvement proved most handy in the Pacific.

The first Lightnings to be deployed for combat duties in the Pacific went to Alaska—respectively Anchorage and Fairbanks in mid-1942. These were only a few P-38Ds and P-38Es that were not actually ready for combat action. But soon, combat-ready P-38Es of the 54th FS, 343rd FG, replaced the handful of noncombatant Lightnings.

In June 1942, the Japanese attacked Kiska Island and the 54th FS relocated its P-38Es to Fort Glenn airstrip on Umnak Island—also in the Aleutian Islands chain. And by July 1943, Lightnings had gained enough air superiority in the region that Japanese forces withdrew. The first kill came on 4 August 1942 when two four-engined flying boats were downed by Lt. S. A. Long and Lt. K. Ambrose—both flying P-38Es. The 343rd FG was assigned to the 11th Air Force and remained in Alaska until VJ Day, and by then, its FSs had been re-equipped with much improved P-38Gs.

As far as the South Pacific went, in mid-1942, P-38Fs of the 39th FS, 35th FG, began arriving in Australia and soon, were moved to Port Moresby, Papua. With the loss of one P-38F on 27 December 1942, the 39th FS claimed eleven enemy aircraft in its first all-out confrontation.

This photo, taken in the fall of 1944 at Mokolea, illustrates what outdoor maintenance was like. This 72nd FS P-38L-1 (S/N 44-24008), perched atop aero stands, is undergoing landing gear tests after being repaired. Note the sign *Tormo's Turbos* on the nose for the plane's crew chief airman Tormo. *Robert F. Dorr Collection*

In the China-Burma-India (CBI) theater, P-38Hs of the 459th FS, 80th FG, began operations in September 1943, first with the 10th AF and finally with the 14th AF. Further, as time went on, the 33rd FG and 51st FG entered combat in the CBI theater. By war's end their P-38Hs had been replaced with both P-38Js and P-38Ls.

Back in late 1942 and early 1943, the 8th FG and 49th FG arrived in New Guinea, and the 18th FG and 347th FG went to Guadalcanal. Respectively, equipped with P-38F and P-38Gs, these groups belonged to the 5th and 13th Air Force commands.

Amazingly, one Fighter Group of the 5th AF, the 475th FG, produced the three top-scoring aces of World War II. These aces—Maj. Dick Bong, Maj. Tom McGuire, and Col. C. H. MacDonald, accounted for 105 enemy aircraft lost by themselves; that is, 40 for Bong, 38 for McGuire and 27 for MacDonald. Exclusively flying P-38s, 38 others became aces as well.

Interestingly, while demonstrating longer-range techniques to 475th FG pilots in the summer of 1944, Charles Lindbergh flew some combat missions while serving as a United Aircraft Corporation technical representative. And on 28 July, while flying a P-38J, he was credited with shooting down a Mitsubishi Ki-51 in the Netherlands East Indies. The joke of it was, since the "Lone Eagle" was not heavily-trained as a combat pilot, that he truly was "Lucky Lindy."

After three full years of heavy-duty combat in World War II, mid-1942 to mid-1945, the P-38 Lightning and its F-4 and F-5 Photo Lightning counterparts had overcome the moans and groans of those who had once feared them. They were indeed radical when they first arrived in 1941 and 1942, but when their users got fully acquainted with them through excellent flight- and combat-training, they became very respectful of them and thankful they had them.

NEXT PAGES
This P-38H-1 (S/N 42-66605) and the other three shown have just been picked up from Lockheed and are on their way to their theater of operation. The H model was a favorite of its pilots and had a top speed of 402 mph at 25,000 feet. *Robert F. Dorr Collection*

A late production P-38E (S/N 41-2257) that had an unknown mishap is shown off-shore in Northern California, circa early 1942. Belonging to the 14th FG then based at Hamilton Field, this E model was to later go to Alaska. *Robert F. Dorr Collection*

Conclusion

More than 10,000 P-38s, F-4s, and F-5s—18 distinct models—were manufactured during World War II. And despite its problems, the Lightning became one of the most formidable combat aircraft of its day.

Lightning first struck when a P-38F knocked down a four-engined Focke-Wulf Condor patrol bomber over Iceland shortly after the United States entered the war. Pilots in Pacific Ocean areas found the vaunted Japanese Zero easy pickings for a fighter with the P-38s ability to shell out 409 rounds per minute of both .50 calibre and 20mm ammunitions. The result was that P-38s shot down more Japanese aircraft than any other fighter.

In Europe the P-38 proved more than a match for the Messerschmitt 109 and Focke-Wulf 190 fighters. And F-4s and F-5s obtained 90 percent of the aerial film in Europe.

The P-38's claims to fame included the first round-trip mission to Berlin by United Kingdom–based fighters and the shooting down of Admiral Isoroku Yamamoto's transport plane. The P-38 was used exclusively by the two top-scoring American pilot aces, USAAF Majors Dick Bong and Tom McGuire. And Charles Lindbergh shot down a Japanese fighter with a P-38 while the famed flier was serving as a civilian field service representative. The Lightning's two turbosupercharged engines were often considered "the round-trip ticket home . . ." to fighter pilots. One P-38 pilot came home 300 miles after a head-on collision with an Me-109. He was flying on one engine, with both tails completely ripped apart and one boom shredded by the impact.

Another P-38 pilot came back from escorting B-17s in a raid over Germany with one engine

This P-38 skinned its nose after the nose landing gear collapsed when the plane hit a muddy hole while landing at Dobodura, New Guinea, on 5 April 1943. Named *Elsie*, this P-38F was operated by the 431st FS, 475th FG of the 5th AF. *USAF via Jeff Ethell*

This photo of then Lt. Dick Bong was taken on 6 March 1943 at his base in New Guinea. From Poplar, Wisconsin, Bong, after becoming America's all-time highest scoring ace with forty confirmed kills, joined Lockheed flight-test operations after the war. Tragically, while testing an early production P/F-80A Shooting Star, the engine quit at low altitude and he was killed in the crash that followed. *USAF via Jeff Ethell*

Aleutian Islands based P-38Es begin their takeoff rolls to patrol for enemy activities off the shore of Alaska in early 1942. These Es belonged to the 54th FS, 343rd FG, 11th AF and were based at Longview Field on Adak Island. *USAF via Jeff Ethell*

The last version of the "plane with two tails" was the P-38M Night Lightning which had just entered service when the war ended. Some 37 mph faster than the Northrop P-61 Black Widow, the P-38M was capable of 406 mph at 15,000 feet. Shown is a P-38M created from a P-38L-5-LO (s/n 44-27234). *Lockheed Martin*

Crew members of the 459th FS (the Twin Dragons) are being briefed before taking off on yet another mission over enemy territory. These 10th AF, 80th FG P-38s were based at Chittagong, India, in January 1945. *USAF via Jeff Ethell*

shot out, five direct 20mm cannon round hits from engine to tail, more than 100 machine gun slug holes, trim tabs shot away, and a vertical stabilizer blown away. The pilot was unscathed.

As it turned out, it was more than good fortune that the Allied forces had P-38s available for combat. Having flown more than 130,000 missions during the war, it was proved that Lightning can and will strike twice in the same place.

After a slow production start of only 266 Lightning aircraft built through 1941, the Lockheed Aircraft Corporation and the Consolidated-

Vultee Aircraft Corporation produced another 9,772 aircraft by war's end for a grand total of 10,038 airplanes.

During four years of combat the Lightning metamorphosed from an unreliable and undesirable contender to a reliable and desirable champion. And during a two-year span of combat action (mid-1942 to mid-1944), no less than forty-one aces had been created while piloting their P-38s. Consider this, with forty and thirty-eight confirmed kills respectively, Majors Bong and McGuire remain America's leading aces.

Since combat pilots heavily depend on their compasses to navigate their fighters safely through missions, it is very important that the fighter's compass is accurate. Here at base in North Africa, a USAAF engineering company surveyed and marked off true north and other points on the compass. As shown here, a 12th AF P-38 has had its compass calibrated, and a tractor is just beginning to tow it away from its wheel stops. *USAF via Jeff Ethell*

Finally, with the advent of the P-38 Lightning, it was demonstrated that an airplane does not have to be of the status quo to be successful. And even though the XP-38 was far ahead of its contemporaries when it appeared in early 1939, and its following variants went through a variety of developmental woes, it proved that the farsightedness of an airframe contractor often can and will prevail. In this case, as with many following aircraft types, it was the Lockheed Aircraft Corporation (now Lockheed Martin Corporation) and its many farseeing employees. One of them especially, the now late Kelly Johnson, who designed some forty aircraft for Lockheed, saw further than others. He proved that a long time ago with the design of his radical XP-38, a fighter airplane that was never overtaken by the progress for which it itself had become a symbol.

Postscript

Of the 10,038 Lightnings delivered and accepted through August 1945, one was delivered in 1939, three were accepted in 1940, 207 were delivered in 1941, 1,478 were accepted in 1942, 2,497 were delivered in 1943, 4,186 were accepted in 1944, and 1,666 were delivered in 1945. Beginning with the XP-38 at the cost of $163,000 in 1938, and decreasing steadily at $134,280 1939–41, $120,407 in 1942, $105,567 in 1943, $97,147.00 in 1944, and finally the cost of a P-38 had dramatically decreased to $95,150 in 1945. Yet, during an all-out war, they were all priceless.

A ground crewman of the 94th FS, 1st FG, poses in his self-styled automobile made from salvaged P-38 parts, including an external auxiliary fuel drop tank with wheels added as well as a plexiglass windscreen. Shown is a P-38L-5-LO (S/N 44-25734) based in Italy, circa early 1945. *USAF via Jeff Ethell*

Here a P-38H is serviced during a visit to the 91st BG base at Bassingbourne, England, on 15 April 1943. Though later versions of the P-47 and P-51 were able to fly long-range escort missions with B-17s and B-24s, it was the early versions of the P-38 that could do it all along. This was a most important aspect of the war, and without these escort fighters, USAAF bombardment aircraft would have literally been sitting ducks in Germany's heavily defended airspace. *USAF via Jeff Ethell*

This is a P-38H-5-LO (S/N 42-67091) of the 71st FS, 1st FG in North Africa. It is being rearmed and refueled for yet another mission against the axis powers in the MTO. Note man on oil drum cleaning the bores of the Lightning's machine guns and cannon. *Kenneth M. Sumney via Jeff Ethell*

Following VE Day, somewhere in Germany, these P-38s of the 430th FS, 474th FG, taxi for takeoff on 20 April 1945 for a sweep mission over the German countryside. *USAF via Jeff Ethell*

This P-38L-5 Lightning (S/N 44-27183), owned by Dave Boyd, is on display at Yanks Air Museum, Chino, California. It now carries registration number N517PA. *Robert F. Dorr Collection*

APPENIDIX
P-38 FIGHTER GROUPS, SQUADRONS, AND COMMANDS

Group	Squadron	Command	Nickname/Motto
1st		8th, 12th, and 15th AFs	
	27th		Fighting Eagles
	71st		Iron Men
	94th		Hat-in-the-Ring Gang
8th		5th AF	
	35th		Black Panthers
	36th		Flying Fiends
	80th		Headhunters
14th		8th, 12th, and 15th AFs	
	37th		
	48th		
	49th		
	50th		Rattlesnakes
18th		5th AF	
	12th		IN OMNI APPARATUS- (Prepared For All Things)
	44th		Bats
	70th		Knights
		419th NFS	
20th		8th AF	
	55th		
	77th		
	79th		Tigers
21st		7th AF	
	46th		Sabre-tooth Tigers
	72nd		PAX PER AUXILIA PARATA-(Peace Through Readiness)
	531st		Strike and Return
33rd		10th and 13th AFs	
	58th		
	59th		Lions
	60th		Crows
35th		5th AF	
	39th		Cobras
	40th		Fighting Fortieth

Group	Squadron	Command	Nickname/Motto
49th		5th AF	
	7th		
	8th		Black Sheep
	9th		
51st		14th AF	
	25th		Daggers
	449th		Falcons
55th		8th AF	
	38th		DUCIMUS CETERI SEQUUNTUR-(We Lead)
	338th		Panthers
	343rd		Ravens
	78th	8th AF	
	82nd		Vikings
	83rd		Lightning Bolts
84th			
80th		10th and 14th AFs	
	459th		
81st		8th, 12th, and 15th AF	
	95th		
	96th		Fighting Jack Rabbits
		97th	Devil-Cats
		97th	
318th	7th AF		Green Dragons
		6th NFS	Game Cocks
	19th		
	44th		
	73rd		
		333rd NFS	
329th		4th AF	
	330th		King Bees
	331st		Griffins
	332nd		White Eagles
	337th		

Group	Squadron	Command	Nickname/Motto
343rd		11th AF	
	11th		Bulls; INFERNE IMIMUS
	18th		Foxes
	54th		Leopards
	344th		
347th		13th AF	
	67th		
	68th		
	339th		Silver Dragons
360th		4th AF	
	371st		
	372nd		
	373rd		
	446th		
364th		8th AF	
	383rd		White Rabbits
	384th		Red Devils
	385th		Pea Shooters
367th		9th AF	
	392nd		
	393rd		
	394th		Bulldogs
370th		9th AF	
	401st		
	402nd		
	485th		
475th		5th AF	Satan's Angels
	431st		Hades
	432nd		Possum
	433rd		Clover
479th		8th AF	
	434th		Red Devils
	435th		
	436th		SEMPER PRIMUS-(First Always)
481st	5th AF		
		421st NFS	
		547th NFS	
		550th NFS	

Note: The 329th and 360th groups were Tactical Groups (TG) and its squadrons were Tactical Squadrons (TS); the acronym NFS means Night Fighter Squadron.

F-4 AND F-5 PHOTOGRAPHIC RECONNAISSANCE GROUPS, SQUADRONS, AND COMMANDS

Group	Squadron	Command	Nickname/Motto
3rd		12th and 15th AFs	
	5th		
	12th		
	23rd		
4th		13th AF	
	17th		Sharks
	38th		
5th		12th and 15th AFs	
	15th		Kingfishers
	32nd		
	37th		
6th		5th AF	
	8th		Eight Ballers
	25th		Thereons
	26th		
7th		8th AF	
	13th		Black Cats
	14th		
	22nd		
	27th		Bat Men
10th		9th AF	
	30th		
	31st		
	33rd		
	34th		
67th		9th AF	
	33rd		

BIBLIOGRAPHY

Angelucci, Enzo with Bowers, Peter. *The American Fighter From 1917 to the Present*. New York, NY: Orion Books, 1987.

Bodie, Warren M. *The Lockheed P-38 Lightning*. Hiawassee. GA: Widewing Publications, 1991.

Davis, Larry. *P-38 Lightning in Action*. Carrollton. TX: Squadron/Signal Publications, Inc., 1990.

Ethell, Jeffrey L. *P-38 Lightning in World War II Color*. Osceola, WI: Motorbooks International Publishers & Wholesalers, 1994.

Grantham, A. Kevin. *P-Screamers: The History of the Surviving Lockheed P-38 Lightnings*. Missoula, MT: Pictorial Histories Publishing Company, Inc., 1994.

LeVier, Tony with Guenther, John. *Pilot*. New York, NY: Bantam Books, 1990.

O'Connell, Jr., Charles F. *First Fighter: A History of America's First Team 1918-1983*. Langley, VA: Office of TAC History, 1987.

Wagner, Ray. *American Combat Planes*. Garden City, NY: Doubleday & Company, Inc., 1982.

Hangar Flying. Burbank, CA: Lockheed Aircraft Corporation, 1942-1944.

Pilots Manual for Lockheed P-38 Lightning. Appleton, WI: Aviation Publications.

INDEX